Walter Ralegh's Virginia

Roanoke Island and the Lost Colony

Solitude Press

Walter Ralegh's Virginia
Roanoke Island and the Lost Colony

ISBN-10   1-928874-08-8
ISBN-13   978-1-928874-08-9

Printed in the United States of America

Image credits provided at end of book

Published by:
Solitude Press
212 Brooks Street
Williamsburg VA 23185

To Ann
for her love, encouragement and support

Contents

Author's Note

First, a word about the spelling of Sir Walter Ralegh's surname. The spelling I have used is the one that he favored. The usual modern spelling, Raleigh, will be more familiar to readers. I use that spelling only when referring to Fort Raleigh, the site of the National Park Service operation on Roanoke Island.

Numerous well-respected historians have written histories of the English settlement of North Carolina's Outer Banks. As in any history, succeeding writers have drawn on the works that came before. I have done likewise, and I want to acknowledge a number of those authorities whose work underlies this new book.

Richard Hakluyt, an English minister who lived through the exciting times in which the Roanoke Island story is set, must come first. Hakluyt had an intense love of the stories of exploration by the English and by the other nations that preceded the English in colonization of North and South America. His *The principal navigations, voyages and discoveries of the English nation* must be the starting place for any serious study of the Roanoke Island settlements. Hakluyt's important contribution is his compilation of hundreds of first-person accounts of voyages of discovery, privateering, and naval battles. Although the stories tend to be told dispassionately, one can imagine the terrible hardships endured by these early mariners and explorers.

Next, David Beers Quinn, with his wife Alison, contributed immeasurably to our knowledge of the early explorations of North America by the Portuguese, Spanish, French and English. The

Quinns' scholarship established the gold standard for research into the exploration and settlement of Roanoke Island. Their books published by the Hakluyt Society, University of North Carolina Press and other publishers provide the best available synthesis of the Hakluyt material with numerous other primary sources discovered and interpreted by the Quinns. I met and was charmed by David and Alison when they were working on David's popular *Set Fair for Roanoke, Voyages and Colonies, 1584-1606*. They lived with my family for many months while in America completing that project and lecturing at various colleges and universities.

Ivor Noel Hume, noted archaeologist and historian, followed the work of the Quinns with insightful, interpretive work based on more recent discoveries, particularly archaeological discoveries that related to the Roanoke Island settlement directly and indirectly. His *The Virginia Adventure, Roanoke to James Towne, An Archaeological and Historical Odyssey*, published nine years after *Set Fair for Roanoke*, provided new insight into the difficulties faced by the Roanoke Island settlers and presents this material in Noel Hume's masterful storytelling style.

Finally, Karen Ordahl Kupperman has contributed greatly to our understanding of the English attempt to settle in North America. Her *Indians and English: Facing off in Early America* provides a thorough grounding for any student of this period of American history and her work substantially expands the treatment of Roanoke Island done by earlier historians.

Anyone interested in Roanoke Island should read the extensive material impressively presented by the National Park Service at their Fort Raleigh

Internet site. Their *Roanoke Revisited Heritage Education Program*, compiled by lebame houston (she prefers lowercase) and Wynne Dough, provides a full series of papers on various topics ranging from biographies of key people such as Sir Walter Ralegh to descriptions of the ships in which the earlier visitors to Roanoke Island sailed.

I want to thank Jim Horn, director of the Rockefeller Research Center of the Colonial Williamsburg Foundation, Thad Tate, former director of the Institute of Early American History and Culture, Milagros Flores, historian at Fort Raleigh National Park, and lebame houston, Elizabethan scholar with the Roanoke Island Historical Association, for reading this manuscript and contributing numerous corrections and their insights into the tale of Roanoke Island and the Lost Colonists. Williamsburg writers Sally Stiles, Kit Fournier and Ann Loker applied their editing skills to my manuscript, and I am grateful for their help.

One final note: The Prolog of this book presents an interpretation of an act of privateering carried out by one of the important English mariners, Sir John Hawkins. The contemporary account of the capture of a Portuguese ship at sea is typically brief. I have expanded that event to a few pages to give the reader a better sense of what it would have felt like to the men on either "end of the cutlass." In extrapolating from the brief historical documentation, I have made a number of deductions: the time it would take one ship to overtake another; the reaction a simple Portuguese mariner would have when learning he had been captured by one of the most notorious privateers of his day; the tactics available when confronted by a vastly superior vessel; and the treatment the prey could expect from Sir John Hawkins if he surrendered peacefully. I believe those deductions are well-grounded, having drawn on other first person accounts of privateering or piracy and other accounts of Sir John Hawkins' behavior. Often a show of force was all that was necessary, but when force met opposing force, the result would be a bloody encounter, as Christopher Newport learned first hand (pun intended).

This book begins with other nations' explorations and colonization efforts well before England finally began to flex her new maritime muscles, and it also deals with privateers or pirates because many if not most of the principal figures involved in the settlement of Roanoke Island engaged in piracy as a matter of course when sailing with colonists to the New World, and many of them had extensive experience in the highly profitable English pastime of privateering in the sixteenth century.

Aleck Loker, Williamsburg, Virginia

Prolog

The year was 1567. They had run before the wind all night trying to leave the other ship in their wake, but as the captain looked astern in the early morning light, the ship was still there—closer than ever. His Portuguese caravel with its three masts and broad bottom was built for quickly sailing along the Iberian coast, carrying wine, fish and other cargo. If he had stayed closer to the coast, he could have run into shallow waters and evaded the much larger, deeper-draft ship that was bearing down on him. But he was sailing with a full load of salted fish, and the North African coast was two hundred miles to port. He knew that, if the wind held, his ship would be overtaken by the other one before he could reach land. His ten men would be no match for the much larger crew on the ship that was slowly but steadily closing on him.

As the sun rose to port, the captain could see more details of the ship. Yesterday morning, it had been a speck on the horizon. As the day wore on, he could see that the ship was bearing for him and he could see that it was much larger than his. Now he could count the sails and see that it was much more heavily armed than his little merchant vessel. His four swivel guns would be no match for the seven or more cannons projecting from the starboard side of the approaching ship—an older design known as a carrack. His only hope would be that the weather would turn nasty before the ship could come within firing range, and he could elude the carrack during a storm or in the dark of night. But it didn't look as if he would make it to nightfall before the big ship closed the gap, and, as he scanned the horizon, the sky was bright blue with no sign of an impending storm.

The Portuguese captain wouldn't delude himself into thinking the big ship would merely sail by. In these parts of the Atlantic, most armed ships sailing this way were looking for prey. They were pirates— they preferred to be called privateers—but they were pirates as far as most Portuguese seamen were concerned. The ship could be English, Dutch or French, but more than likely it wasn't just a cargo vessel. From bitter experience, he knew the odds were that this was a heretic pirate from one of those countries come to prey on a poor, honest Catholic mariner such as himself.

As the morning wore on, the captain saw someone on the other ship looking at him, and now he could make out about a dozen of the crewmen on the carrack's deck. They held muskets as they leaned against the rail, waiting for their captain to give them the order to fire. The crew on the caravel looked back at the ship with fear, awaiting the first shot and wondering what their fate would be. They wouldn't have long to wait. The two ships were now within a mile of each other. The captain of the caravel knew that before the sun reached its zenith, the big ship would be within gun range. There was little he could do to prepare. He had already ordered his men to hide what little gold they had in the compartment he had built into the ceiling of his cabin. Hopefully, the pirates wouldn't find that. There was nothing he could do to protect the cargo of fish. Those casks would probably be aboard the superior vessel before night.

Now he could see the English ensign flying from the stern of the approaching ship, and a long red pennant with a white cross flying from the main masthead. He hoped this English captain's ship was well-provisioned and manned by a healthy crew and not a ship of sick and starving men who would show no mercy in their desperate attempt to find food and water as well as valuable cargo. He would know soon enough. The Portuguese helmsman looked back nervously and let the bow of the caravel fall off a few points, causing their speed to drop. The captain hollered at him to mind his course or he'd get them all killed. The helmsman quickly brought them back onto their heading and he felt the ship vibrate slightly beneath his feet as it regained speed.

But, try as he might, the captain could not get enough speed from his ship to outrun the pursuing pirate. He could see the men in the English ship now standing more alert, checking their weapons and waiting for the order to fire. He knew that this ship's captain had no intention of sailing by with a friendly salute. He meant to rob the caravel. The Portuguese captain told his men to pray to the Virgin for gentle treatment by the pirates. There was nothing else to be done. He bowed his head and made a silent prayer that he and his men would be allowed to live and sail back to Porto.

When he looked up, the English ship had turned slightly to starboard, bringing her port side into view at a distance of about two hundred yards. He saw the puff of black smoke from the muzzle of a cannon amidships and then heard the boom of the charge only a fraction of a second before a nine-pound cannon ball ripped through his main sail. He felt his ship lurch as the cannon ball tore through the sail, straining the standing rigging supporting the mast. If there had been any doubt about the other captain's intentions, there was none now.

He ordered his helmsman to bring the caravel into the wind and ordered another man to lower the ensign flying at his ship's stern.

The English captain ordered his men to hold their fire as they quickly closed on the caravel, now sitting still in the ocean swells with its sails luffing in the strong breeze. The English captain gave orders to maneuver his 700-ton ship alongside the caravel—a difficult maneuver in the rolling seas—and lower most of her sails to reduce her speed. As he sailed up to the caravel floating much lower in the water, he ordered lines cast to the captured prize and gave orders to the Portuguese captain to make his ship fast against the hull of the English vessel. As the two ships were lashed together, the Portuguese captain had his men lower their luffing sails and allowed his ship to be carried along by the much bigger vessel. He wondered what would happen next.

He didn't have long to wait. The English captain invited him to come aboard and had his sailors lower a rope ladder for the Portuguese captain to use. As soon as he was on deck, the interrogation began. Where was he from? What was his cargo? Where was he bound? Fortunately, the English captain had a Portuguese pilot on board and they were easily able to communicate through the pilot's translation. This made it less likely there would be any misunderstanding between them; it also made it harder for the Portuguese captain to withhold information and blame it on a language problem. The English captain ordered his men to begin removing the cargo from the hold of the caravel as he continued to question his "guest."

"Aye Captain Hawkins," replied the man in charge of the boarding party.

The Portuguese captain felt a chill run up his spine when he heard that name. Hawkins was well-known and feared by the Portuguese who traded in African slaves. Hawkins had a nasty reputation of taking what he wanted and not shying away from using strong measures to get it. He had wiped out whole villages and sent the natives fleeing for their lives into the bush when they tried to thwart him. He delighted in attacking Portuguese slavers in the African rivers, wrecking their ships, stealing their human cargoes, and selling them in the Caribbean to the Spaniards. The Portuguese captain knew he had better not provoke this man.

The boarding party made quick work of hoisting the casks of fish onto the deck of the English ship where they were just as quickly lowered into the empty hold. It was clear that the Portuguese captain had the misfortune to be one of the first prizes captured on this voyage. A few of the Englishmen remained on the caravel, rummaging through all the spaces in their search for other valuables. They returned to the English ship with a couple bottles of brandy and some pewter plates they had found in the captain's cabin, but no gold.

The Englishman allowed the Portuguese captain to return to his ship. He doubted the Portuguese had anything else of much value. It was time to be free of the rather insignificant prize and get on his way to the real aim of this venture: a trip to Africa to pick up slaves and then a cruise through the Spanish Caribbean trading slaves for hides, ginger and any other marketable items they could lay their hands on. Of course, his greatest hope—and that of his backers back in Plymouth—was to catch a Spanish treasure galleon as it sailed back to Spain in the late summer laden with American gold and silver. That would make all his other profits insignificant by comparison.

A single treasure ship could contain enough gold to make many men instantly wealthy. And, according to the rules of the privateering trade, every member of the crew would share in one-third of the wealth they brought back to England after the crown took one-fifth of any Spanish or Portuguese treasure seized by the privateers. The rest would be divided equally between the ship's owner and the backers of the venture. The possibility of great wealth drove these adventurers to take substantial risks during a six-month or longer voyage into the cauldron that was called the Caribbean or the West Indies.

The Portuguese captain said a silent prayer of thanks to the Virgin as he climbed down the rope ladder into his swaying but undamaged ship. He ordered his men to cast his ship loose from the pirate ship and raise their sails. Soon the caravel was headed east, away from the quickly disappearing English vessel, and every man aboard knew that they had been lucky to escape real harm. Their now-empty ship sailed nimbly over the swells as the Portuguese captain set a course up the African coast. As he looked back, he read the name on the stern of the English Ship: *Jesus of Lubeck.* What a blasphemy, he thought—such a holy name for such an unholy enterprise.

While this episode was of serious consequences to the poor Portuguese captain, it barely rated notice in an account of Sir John Hawkins' third voyage to the New World written many years later by one of the survivors of that ill-fated trip. In Hawkins'

personal account of the voyage, he doesn't even mention the capture of the caravel, giving evidence to how insignificant the routine capture of such a trifling prize was in that age of privateers.

Some captures at sea were considerably more violent. Later in this Roanoke story we'll see that one English privateer—later a hero of the Virginia Company—lost an arm while boarding a Spanish treasure ship. In fact, men earned well-established bonuses for the loss of arms, legs, and eyes in the course of piracy.

Whether you were a privateer or pirate depended very much on which end of the cutlass you were on. To the Portuguese and Spanish seaman killed, maimed or captured by the English during the sixteenth century, men like Hawkins were clearly pirates, brigands, and bandits. Yet men like Hawkins would bring the first English settlers to the New World.

Chapter 1
The Age of Exploration

According to a National Park Service publication, "To say simply that English piracy flourished during the last half of the sixteenth century is a gross understatement of the situation. It had, in fact, achieved the status of a recognized profession."

The Englishmen who practiced the privateering profession—men such as Francis Drake, Walter Ralegh, and Richard Grenville—viewed themselves as patriotic English subjects merely carrying out the foreign policy of Queen Elizabeth while opening up the lucrative trade opportunities in the New World to their countrymen. England had no colonies in North America, and it would be 1585 before she made a serious attempt at settling Roanoke Island, and 1607 before she finally planted a permanent settlement in the New World at Jamestown. In the meantime, men like Hawkins saw nothing wrong with relieving the Spaniards of some of the treasures they had stolen from the native inhabitants of the New World. They certainly had some reason to feel justified.

To understand how England came so late to colonizing the New World, first we need to see what other countries had accomplished in the nearly one hundred years since Columbus had stepped ashore in the New World.

More than 200 years before Columbus, Venetian and Genoese traders had sailed through the Bosporus Strait and crossed the Black Sea, establishing a port on the Crimean peninsula convenient to caravans trading in the Orient. Columbus claimed to be Genoese, but he sailed for the King and Queen of Spain who financed and equipped his fleet of three ships. His discovery of lands across the Atlantic Ocean in 1492 was the logical extension of many preceding voyages during the fifteenth century that expanded western Europeans' knowledge of their world. In all probability, Columbus was not the first mariner to visit the New World, but his voyage marks the first historically documented visit to the Caribbean.

Long before Columbus opened Europe's eyes to the New World, Portuguese explorers had, through a series of voyages beginning in the early fifteenth century, extended the practical trade routes by sea to India and the orient. Four years before Columbus's voyage to the west, Bartholomeu Dias finally rounded the tip of Africa, culminating seventy-five years of gradually expanding Portuguese explorations along the African coast. As with most technology, significant advances came very slowly at first, but then achievements came more rapidly. By 1497, Vasco da Gama sailed from Portugal, rounded the tip of Africa—the Cape of Good Hope—and sailed up to India.

The Portuguese established a foothold in the African coastal regions that gave them an initial trading advantage—particularly trading in African slaves. When they reached the Indian Ocean, the Portuguese had found a sea route to the riches of the orient, particularly the much sought-after spices, avoiding the dangerous overland crossing through lands that the Ottoman Turks had controlled for more than a century. This gave them a great advantage over other European powers.

Spain's sponsorship of Columbus tilted the board in their direction, and they quickly capitalized on their achievement by signing with Portugal the

Treaty of Tordesillas in 1494. This treaty, blessed by Pope Alexander VI (a sixty-two year old Spaniard), divided the world into a Portuguese-controlled enterprise to the east and a Spanish enterprise to the west. The dividing line was a meridian (line of longitude) in the Atlantic, approximately 1,000 miles to the west of the Cape Verde Islands, which lie off the west coast of Africa. As it turned out, that line left most of South America within the Portuguese empire, and all of central and North America was designated as exclusively Spanish territory as far as the Pope was concerned. At that time, all Western European Christians were essentially Roman Catholic, but with Martin Luther's protestations in 1517, a new dynamic called the Reformation began to affect Europe and the political balance of power.

Columbus was convinced that he had landed in the easternmost portions of Asia, and, wrong though he was, many believed that he had found another sea route to the valuable spices and silks of the Orient. Within a few years, most geographers believed that Columbus had found a new land, but they continued in their belief that this new land was somehow joined to or very close to Asia. That led to various expeditions to locate a maritime passage through the new land to the South Sea, now known as the Pacific Ocean. The Spaniards soon found a practical overland portage from the Caribbean to the Pacific at what is now known as the Isthmus of Panama, and Magellan showed how ships could sail around South America and reach the Pacific, albeit with a great deal of difficulty and hardship. (He died there in 1521 before his ship completed the first documented circumnavigation of the Earth).

Spain's View of North America as a nearly exclusive Spanish domain in the 16th Century

The Spanish quickly capitalized on their newly acquired treasure trove in the West Indies by establishing Spanish ports on the major islands such as Hispaniola (modern-day Haiti and Dominican Republic) and Cuba, and, soon thereafter, ports on the Bay of Campeche in modern-day Mexico, the Yucatan peninsula and the Gulf of Darien (Panama).

Spain made slaves of the Indians they found there, and after stealing as much of the Indian gold as they could find and melting it down into ingots for shipment to Spain, they began to extract and refine raw gold and silver from the Indian mines. Soon they had established a pipeline of gold and silver flowing in astronomical proportions into Spanish coffers.

England made a brief attempt at expansion into the New World in 1497 when John Cabot (Giovanni Cabota, yet another Italian) sailed to the northwest, landing somewhere near Newfoundland on June 24, 1497, and claiming the land for England, the country that had given him the opportunity to make the voyage. He was accompanied by his English-born son Sebastian; they sailed along the coast (now Canada) looking unsuccessfully for a passage to the Pacific Ocean and Asia. Cabot concluded incorrectly that he had reached the Asian mainland. His voyage, although it accomplished little in terms of goading England into a more concerted effort to settle parts of the New World, was important as it formed the basis for later English claims with regard to North America, which the Spanish viewed as their exclusive territory.

According to renowned archaeologist, historian and writer Ivor Noel Hume, an Englishman made an early attempt at establishing a colony in North America in 1517:

[John] *Rastell, a printer and publisher by trade, seems to have lacked any prior maritime experience. Nevertheless, he chose to command the fleet himself. That was a mistake. Supplied with a protective patent from the king* [Henry VIII] *dated March 5, 1517, and led by the ships* Barbara *and* Mary Barking, *his flotilla left London in the spring of that year, bound, as the patent put it, for "distant parts of world, remote from our Kingdom of England." The parts proved less remote than expected, for the expedition got no farther than Cork on the southern coast of Ireland.*

Noel Hume explained that the ships' crews put Rastell out in Ireland because he refused to go off on a trading or pirating jaunt along the French coast rather than sail for North America to establish his colony. Rastell's experience with an uncooperative and uncommitted crew typifies the situation the Roanoke Island settlers would be confronted with. England would make no more attempts at colonization of the New World for nearly sixty years.

For their part, the French made their first foray into North America in 1524 when Giovanni da Verrazano (another Italian) sailing for King Francis I explored the middle latitudes of North America from Florida to Maine (in modern-day terms). Giovanni's brother converted his meticulous logbook notations into a map in 1529. Now, France had a claim on North America as well. The Verrazano map included a detail that would intrigue explorers for more than 80 years: the map showed a deep bay off the Pacific Ocean penetrating the continent to nearly the Atlantic Ocean in the mid-Atlantic area. Explorers would make many fruitless attempts to find this mythical Northwest Passage in the hopes of establishing a safe and economical route to the western ocean and the riches of the orient.

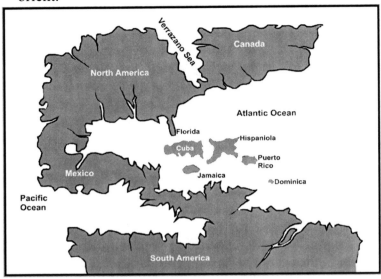

The Concept of the New World in the mid-16th Century
The Verrazano Sea would become the mythical Northwest Passage

France's next attempt at securing a place in North American settlement came in 1562 when Jean Ribault landed near present-day Jacksonville, Florida, took possession for the King of France and, on an island in the St. John's River, erected a column with the coat of arms of the Queen of France. Ribault met with the local Timucuan Indians and exchanged trade goods for food. He then sailed up the coast to a spot near Parris Island, South Carolina and built a small log fortification he named Charlesfort, in honor of King Charles IX, leaving thirty soldiers to hold the fort until his return.

Although Spain had no settlements at that time in Florida or elsewhere on the east coast, they claimed all of North America as part of their lands, citing the Pope's ratification of the Treaty of Tordesillas to justify their position. The Frenchman, Ribault—a Huguenot Protestant—was considered a heretic by the Catholic Spanish. To complicate matters, Roman Catholic Catherine de Medici, mother of French King Charles IX, had felt it her duty to warn Philip II of Spain that French Huguenots were attempting to intrude on the Spanish lands claimed in America. Spain would move quickly to eradicate Ribault's settlement.

The wars of religion had broken out in France pitting Protestants against Catholics, and French colonialists were drawn into that conflict. So Ribault went to England to try to gain support for a second voyage to Charlesfort, but Queen Elizabeth had him arrested to prevent further French ventures. By this time she had Englishmen with designs on building an English outpost in North America. She didn't want Frenchmen as well as Spaniards in the way. Meanwhile, the thirty men left at Charlesfort had argued among themselves and then sailed away in a longboat, abandoning the first French settlement in North America.

Rene Laudonniere, who had been Ribault's deputy on the first voyage, took up the challenge of maintaining a French presence in Florida. He led 300 men with three ships back to Florida in June 1564. The French ships landed on the St. John's River and erected a small fort, called Fort Caroline in honor of the king (whose Latin name was Carolus). The colony consisted of a mix of soldiers and various artisans. But trouble soon erupted, and Laudonniere proved unable to govern the settlers, some of whom set out in boats to try their hand at pirating Spanish gold in the West Indies.

John Hawkins, returning from trading slaves in the West Indies, stopped at Fort Caroline mid-July 1565 and found the Frenchmen in poor condition. In addition to food, he gave them the friendly advice that the Spanish were aware of their colony and were bent on ejecting them. He generously left them with a ship to take them back to France if they decided to evacuate the colony. Hawkins sent a similar warning along with a report on the condition of the Fort Caroline colony to the French court when he returned to England. In response, Jean Ribault, recently released from prison in England, sailed in June 1565 on a relief mission with 600 French settlers and soldiers. This mission included women and children as well as men.

In August he found the Fort Caroline colony in disarray, dispirited and ready to return home. They had made enemies of the local Indians and had failed to work together under Laudonniere's leadership—strikingly similar to later English colonization attempts in Virginia.

Their relief at Ribault's arrival was short lived. Soon, Spaniard Pedro Menendez de Aviles, former Captain General of the Fleet of the West Indies, sailed into the St. John's River bent on executing every Protestant Frenchman he could find. After a confrontation with the five French ships that blocked his entrance to the river, Menendez withdrew to a site about thirty miles down the coast and established an outpost that eventually grew into St. Augustine, Florida. This outpost, with so inauspicious a start, became the oldest continuously occupied European settlement in the United States.

Ribault decided the only way to survive the expected Spanish aggression was to make a pre-emptive strike. Unfortunately, his ships ran into a fierce storm that swept them southward, well past St. Augustine, and most were driven ashore where they were wrecked. Menendez launched an overland attack on Fort Caroline with 500 soldiers. They took three days to slog through the swamps, but arrived at Fort Caroline eager for a fight. They attacked the nearly defenseless settlement early in the morning and killed 142 settlers. Laudonniere escaped with about fifty survivors and made it to the coast. Fort Caroline now became Spanish Fort Mateo.

Menendez then proceeded back to St. Augustine and found Ribault and his men trapped on the seashore south of Matanzas Inlet. Ribault had no recourse but to surrender. After Menendez accepted his surrender, he had Ribault and all of the Protestants among his troop murdered. Ten French Catholics and six cabin boys were spared. This marked the end of France's attempts to settle near Spanish territory on the Atlantic coast of North America.

France achieved success in the New World in 1603 when Samuel de Champlain explored the St. Lawrence River, still looking for a Northwest Passage to the Pacific Ocean and Asia. He returned the next year and sailed along the coast of Nova Scotia, Cape Cod and down the Atlantic Coast to present-day Rhode Island.

In 1605, Champlain was involved in starting a French colony at Nova Scotia (Port Royal), and in 1608 he took about thirty settlers to establish a fur-trading outpost at what became Quebec. Champlain continued to lead and augment this settlement until the English took the fort there in 1629. In 1632, France and England concluded a treaty returning Quebec to the French. Champlain returned to Quebec and served as the governor until his death on Christmas Day 1635.

In 1576, English mariner Martin Frobisher made his first of three voyages to the New World. His original purpose was to find the Northwest Passage to the orient. He left England with three small ships on June 7, but his fleet was soon reduced to one, the *Gabriel* of twenty tons. The other ship, the *Michael*, deserted the expedition and Frobisher's pinnace was lost in the stormy North Atlantic. Frobisher found what he thought was the Northwest Passage at Baffin Island in present-day Canada. The supposed passage is now called Frobisher Bay. While there, Frobisher took a native Inuit (Eskimo) man hostage and returned with him along with supposed gold ore to England. Although the ore eventually proved worthless, the find sparked a shift from seeking the Northwest Passage to a quest for gold mines in the arctic territory of the Inuit people. Two more voyages were made by Frobisher in which he mined for gold and brought more Inuit to England. The three Inuit—a man, woman and child—all succumbed to European diseases. The man and woman were buried at St. Stephen's Church in Bristol in November, 1577. The child died in London soon after and was buried at St. Olave's Church. Frobisher's voyages proved unsuccessful in both respects: he had not found the mythical Northwest Passage, and he had found no gold. But, his voyages had stimulated interest in the northern latitudes of the New World in England.

England finally resumed a somewhat sporadic and disorganized attempt at establishing settlements in the New World about the time John Hawkins returned with news of the French colony at Fort Caroline (1565). One man who would become important in English colonization of the New World was Sir Humphrey Gilbert. Gilbert had served for a couple of years under the Earl of Warwick's English company in the siege of Le Havre at the mouth of the River Seine in the French war. Later he served in the English army in Munster, Ireland, where he received his knighthood in 1570. He represented Plymouth in Parliament the next year. Like many of his West Country associates, he had a desire to search for the fabled Northwest Passage and explore the New World, and he saw the economic advantage for England to have a permanent settlement in North America from which she could gain economic benefits and frustrate Spanish expansion.

On June 11, 1578, English Queen Elizabeth granted Gilbert a six-year patent to establish a settlement in North America between Spanish Florida and the arctic. Gilbert hastily arranged for ships and set sail on September 26, 1578, but fierce storms put a quick end to his attempted voyage.

In 1583, realizing his time was running out, Sir Humphrey Gilbert made another attempt at settlement. On June 11th (one year before the patent would have expired) he sailed with 260 men on five ships: *Delight* (120 tons), *Ralegh* (a bark of 200 tons belonging to Walter Ralegh), *Golden Hind* (a ship of 40 tons, not the famous one of Sir Francis Drake), *Swallow* (a ship of 40 tons), and *Squirrel* (a frigate of 10 tons). Ralegh's ship turned back almost immediately—an unknown illness reportedly had swept through the crew.

Gilbert, now with four ships, reached St. John's, Newfoundland on August 3rd, 1583. Here is how Edward Hayes, one of the commanders of the expedition, characterized England's late entry into the New World:

The first discovery of these coasts (never heard of before) was well begun by John Cabot the father, and Sebastian his son, an Englishman born, who were the first finders out of all that great tract of land stretching from the cape of Florida unto those Islands which we now call the New found land, all which they brought and annexed unto the crown of England. Since when if with like diligence the search of inland countries had been followed, as the discovery upon the coast and outposts there of was performed by those men, no doubt Her Majesty's territories and revenues had been mightily enlarged and advanced by this day.

The English clearly subscribed to the belief that Cabot's voyages had given them a valid claim on most of North America. When Gilbert and his small fleet arrived at St. John's, however, they didn't find an empty country. To the contrary, that area had been used for many years by fishermen of many nations including Portugal and France, and when Gilbert sailed into the harbor he found thirty-six vessels already there. Undaunted, Gilbert landed and officially claimed the land for 200 leagues (about 600 miles) in all directions for Queen Elizabeth. Apparently Gilbert was also unaffected by the sight of cattle roaming freely about the area—the descendants of cattle brought there about thirty years before by the Portuguese.

On the day after their landing, Gilbert decided that law and order, English style, would reign over his new principality, and he ordained the following three laws:

1. The Church of England would be the religion of the land.

2. Any attempt by others to seize his land (as the queen's patentee) would be considered high treason and punishable by death.
3. Anyone speaking of the queen dishonorably or seditiously would have his ears cut off and have his ship and goods confiscated.

Whether the thirty-six ships' captains of various nations paid any attention to Sir Humphrey's ranting is not recorded. Gilbert went on to award titles of ownership to the various harbor-side lands that were currently occupied. In exchange, the owners paid Gilbert rent. On shore, there were various buildings and structures used for the storage of salt, equipment and the preserved fish that was the commodity produced at St. John's by the fleet that plied the banks off of Newfoundland.

Among Gilbert's men were a number of artisans including mineral experts. They reported to him that they had found silver ore. He had their samples placed aboard the *Delight* and insisted that the men keep the find a secret while among the strangers at St. John's.

Some of Gilbert's men had fallen sick; some had also attempted mutiny; still others had disappeared into the wilderness to find another ship to take them home. Gilbert sent the sick men home aboard the *Swallow*. Gilbert's ill-conceived plan to leave men at St. John's to meet the terms of his royal patent failed when he found none willing to remain there through the frigid winter.

He boarded the tiny *Squirrel* and began his exploration of the coast below the fishing settlement. His plan was to replenish his supplies at St. John's and then sail well south to seek a more temperate climate in which to plant a permanent settlement.

On August 20, *Delight, Golden Hind,* and *Squirrel* headed along the southern coast of Newfoundland, covering only a few hundred miles in nine days before *Delight* ran onto shoals and went down, taking most of the remaining members of the expedition and their supplies. Also lost in the wreck were the purported silver ore samples. Gilbert aboard *Squirrel* and Edward Hayes aboard *Golden Hind* attempted to make further progress south, but the weather prevented it. Finally Gilbert said:

> *Be content, we have seen enough, and take no care of expense past, I will set you forth royally the next spring, if God send us safe home. Therefore I pray you let us no longer strive here, where we fight against the elements.*

The two tiny ships headed for home on the last day of August, 1583. The ships kept company through stormy seas for nine days, and then the *Squirrel* slipped beneath the waves during the night. The *Golden Hind* was left to complete the voyage alone, without the sponsor who had failed to establish an occupied settlement in North America and who had died convinced he had found silver in the New World. *Golden Hind* arrived in Falmouth on September 22, 1583 with bad news for Sir John Gilbert and Walter Ralegh, Sir Humphrey Gilbert's brother and half-brother. However, this disastrous first attempt lit a spark within Walter Ralegh that would lead to the planting of a colony in the New World at Roanoke Island. Ralegh would take up the challenge of establishing a permanent English presence in North America, but his challenge would be fraught with political interference, war and a lack of commitment on the part of some of the men he needed to carry out his plans.

Chapter 2
England in the Wider World of the 16th Century

In the mid-sixteenth century, when Queen Elizabeth I came to the throne, England was beginning to look beyond her coasts and see both the economic opportunities in the greater world and the serious risk posed by Spain, the preeminent power in the western world. Spain had catapulted into a position of dominance in Europe on the strength of their newfound riches in the West Indies. Their treasure galleons brought riches from the Orient via the Philippines and across the Isthmus of Panama to join the annual gold and silver convoy to Spain. Also, Spain had moved into the Low Countries and was meddling in internal French politics. Spain had supported the return of the Catholic Queen Mary to the English throne. Mary's short and bloody reign had briefly restored Catholicism, at the suffering of many English Protestants. Then, with Queen Elizabeth, Catholics were again suppressed in England.

These affairs brought Spain under the envious and fearful eyes of the French, Dutch and English who had no such wealth with which to compete in an increasingly inflationary world market. Spain's expansionist tendencies were prompted in part by the rise of what they considered heretical powers in England, France and the Low Countries, as the spread of Protestantism threatened heretofore Roman Catholic kingdoms. Consequently, not only economics but also religion played an important role in the conflicts that erupted between Spain and other European countries in the sixteenth century. Europe was deeply divided by the antagonism between the old Roman Catholic religion and the newly emerging Protestant faiths. The conflict escalated beyond differences over religious practices and spawned various bloody military engagements.

When John Hawkins sailed to Africa and the West Indies on his slave trading missions, he was antagonizing the Spanish—a risky business at that time. His flagship, the *Jesus of Lubeck* belonged to Queen Elizabeth. She had loaned the ship to him knowing full well that he intended to use it and his other ships to sail to Guinea in Africa to take African slaves by force from the Portuguese slavers there and sell them to Spaniards in the West Indies. At times, Hawkins, Drake and other mariners sailed with Letters of Marque from the queen authorizing them to seize cargoes—particularly gold and silver—from Spanish and Portuguese ships. This was overt, intentional aggression against the Spaniards for their attempt to keep the West Indies, in truth the whole of the Americas, as an exclusively Spanish enterprise.

This use of private vessels and mariners to carry out English foreign policy was necessary at that time because the crown had a very small navy with minimal capability. The lure of vast amounts of gold and silver for the taking from the annual Spanish shipments out of the West Indies enticed many Englishmen to participate in sanctioned privateering—legalized piracy. The crown added to the incentive by taking a relatively modest twenty percent of the prizes taken by the privateers. Syndicates of investors in London and Plymouth put up much of the capital to finance the voyages of the privateers. Ship owners stood to gain substantially by permitting their vessels to be used as privateers. And the common seamen stood to gain as well, although they faced the greatest risk and hardship.

Seamen at that time made about ten shillings per month (equal to about $170 today) when they could find work. In the sixteenth century, England was still very much isolated from Europe and had little experience of the New World. They had a small fishing industry and bought many of their fish from Dutch and Portuguese fishermen. They had negligible world trade and consequently few opportunities for men to go to sea to earn a living. People living in England at that time might spend an entire lifetime never straying more than twenty five or fifty miles (one or two day's journey) from their home village. So, the opportunity to go to sea with the exciting prospect of reaping a relatively large reward for their troubles attracted young men to the life of piracy and privateering. Many of these mariners came from the English West Country counties of Cornwall and Devon.

The Englishmen who led the first expeditions to Roanoke Island came from that region, and many of them were related. All of the men who led those first expeditions had divided and, at times, conflicting goals: privateering and colonial settlement.

Hawkins continued his slave trading voyages to the West Indies and, accompanied by his cousin Francis Drake (later the famous Sir Francis), made a fateful trip in 1567-1568. Throughout the West Indies, the Spaniards resisted trading with him as a result of a decree from the king of Spain. Hawkins' cruise ended in all-out war with the Spaniards at San Juan de Ulua on the Mexican coast where the *Jesus of Lubeck* was destroyed and Hawkins and Drake barely escaped. This adventure seriously damaged the already fragile relationship between Philip II of Catholic Spain and Elizabeth I of Protestant England.

In 1571, Hawkins, posing as an English traitor but, in fact, an Elizabethan spy, learned in Spain that King Philip was planning an invasion of England. The Spanish king planned to build a large armada of ships to capture England and restore Roman Catholicism to the English throne. King Philip had political as well as religious reasons to oppose Queen Elizabeth. For five years England and France had supported the Dutch in their revolt against Spanish rule of the Netherlands. England and France wanted to eject Spain from the Low Countries.

For a number of years, England had been sending troops to France to support the Huguenots in their opposition to the Catholics during the Wars of Religion. In 1572 on St. Bartholomew's Day (August 24), French Catholics slaughtered thousands of Huguenots in Paris, leaving the streets awash

Sir Francis Drake

in blood. During the next weeks, perhaps as many as 100,000 Protestants were murdered throughout France. This massacre strengthened the English resolve to weaken Spanish Catholic dominance of Western Europe and the Americas. Concurrently, England was embroiled in controlling a rebellion in

Ireland, and Spain was suspected of assisting Irish rebels.

In 1580, Francis Drake returned triumphantly from a campaign of harassing the Spanish in the West Indies and the Pacific Coast of the Americas, during which he became the first Englishman to circumnavigate the Earth. He had audaciously planted an English flag on the Pacific coast of North America and had proclaimed it the queen's territory of New Albion. He had plundered Spanish towns and galleons and returned to Plymouth with hundreds of pounds of gold, many tons of silver, casks of pearls and jewels stolen from the Spanish. As a reward for these exploits, Queen Elizabeth knighted Drake aboard the *Golden Hind*, much to the chagrin of King Philip of Spain who considered Drake a common criminal. The queen's share of the Spanish plunder kept her solvent for years.

Drake was back in the West Indies a few years later, and England and Spain were officially at war. Drake had a merry time raiding Spanish towns including Santiago, Santo Domingo and Cartagena, as well as destroying St. Augustine in Florida. If he hadn't gotten sick and returned to England in 1586, he would have continued his punitive raids throughout the West Indies.

The next year, with word that Spain had assembled a huge invasion fleet, Drake boldly led a battle force of thirty English ships into the Spanish port of Cadiz and destroyed thirty-three of their war ships. Back in England, Sir Francis Drake was appointed Vice Admiral of the Fleet under Admiral Lord Howard of Effingham. They, along with Sir John Hawkins, Sir Walter Ralegh and many others, made preparations to defend England against the inevitable Spanish invasion. They assembled a huge fleet of 197 English ships of various sizes. They wouldn't have long to wait.

On May 28, 1588, 130 Spanish ships carrying 30,000 men began sailing from the port of Lisbon in Portugal, also ruled by Philip II. Across the channel from England, an additional force of 16,000 men led by the Spanish Duke of Parma was poised to join in the invasion. These were not insignificant armed merchant vessels. The following contemporary account by Emanuel van Meteran gives some idea of just how large some of the Spanish ships were:

The Galeons were 64 in number, being of an huge bigness, and very stately built, being of marveilous force also, and so high, that they resembled great castles, most fit to defend themselves and to withstand any assault, but farre inferiour unto the English and Dutch ships, which can with great dexteritie weild and turne themselves. The upperworke of the said Galeons was of thicknesse and strength sufficient to [ward] off musket-shot. The lower worke and the timbers thereof were out of measure strong, being framed of plankes and ribs foure or five foote in thickness, insomuch that no [cannon balls] could pierce them, but such as were discharged hard at hand [point blank range].

The Galliasses were of such bigness, that they contained within them chambers, chapels, turrets, pulpits, and other commodities of great houses. The Galliasses were rowed with great oares, there being in [each] one of them 300 slaves for the same purpose, and were able to do great service with the force of their Ordinance.

You may be surprised to learn that Spain still used huge ships propelled by oars manned by slaves. According to this account, the Armada depended on the labor of 2,088 slaves.

English and Spanish ships in combat between Dover (right) and Calais (left).

Due to bad weather, the Spanish Armada didn't arrive off the English coast of Cornwall until July 19. As the Armada continued up the coast to Plymouth, 150 English ships put out of port to engage them with Vice Admiral Sir Francis Drake in command. In two skirmishes, neither side could claim victory. The action then moved across the channel to Dunkirk where the Duke of Parma's troops awaited transportation to make their invasion. The ships of the Armada were bottled up in a tight formation, and on the evening of July 28, Drake loaded eight ships with gunpowder and incendiary material, ignited them and set them to drift into the Spanish fleet. The panicked Spanish captains ordered their anchor cables cut as they scrambled to avoid the holocaust drifting toward them. The more maneuverable English ships then preyed on the scattered and disorganized Spaniards. The battle continued to Gravelines on the French coast the next day where the Armada reformed. Eleven of the Spanish ships were destroyed with the loss of about 2,000 men. The English fared much better, losing only a few hundred men in battle, although a typhus outbreak later killed thousands.

The Armada then sailed north, away from the French coast, trailed and harried by the English ships all the way up the North Sea-coast of England to Scotland, where the English finally broke off the chase due to lack of ammunition. The Spaniards suffered great casualties from the stormy seas as they sailed around Scotland and Ireland on their way back to Spain. They arrived home with only sixty-seven of the original 130 ships and had lost about 20,000 men. For a time, England still feared that the Duke of Parma's troops would cross the channel and invade, but that never happened. This victory injected great pride into the English people, giving them more confidence in their growing maritime capability, and Europe saw England as an emerging world power. Sir Francis Drake was hailed as a national hero.

The next year, Drake led a fleet to Spain to destroy their navy and, hopefully, to capture the expected West Indies treasure fleet. Another goal of this assault force was to push the Spanish out of Portugal by supporting a Portuguese claimant to the throne. However, Drake failed on all counts, and crept back to England after taking heavy losses. War with Spain would continue through the rest of Elizabeth's reign, ending when James I, who favored peaceful coexistence with Spain, came to the English throne.

Sir Walter Ralegh had played an important part in the defense of England during the attempted Spanish invasion of 1588. As Vice Admiral and Lord Lieutenant of Cornwall—distinctions Queen Elizabeth had bestowed on her favorite courtier— Ralegh raised a large army of nearly 6,000 men that stood ready to oppose the expected forces of the Duke of Parma. Of course, those troops were never needed in battle. However, Ralegh joined Sir John Hawkins and Sir Francis Drake in the decisive naval battles at Dunkirk and Gravelines. Later Ralegh and Sir Richard Grenville caught twenty Spanish ships in the Irish Sea, attacked them and drove them to their death on the rocky coast. We'll hear more about Ralegh and Grenville as we begin to examine their roles in English colonization of Roanoke Island.

Chapter 3
Sir Walter Ralegh's Rise to Prominence

Walter Ralegh, like many of the other key figures in the story of Roanoke, came from the West Country. He was born in Devonshire about 1554 into a prominent Protestant family. His father, also named Walter, had married Joan Drake, a cousin of Sir Francis Drake. But she died in 1530 and it was Walter's third wife, Katherine Champer-nowne, who was Sir Walter's mother. She had been married to Otto Gilbert, father of Sir Humphrey Gilbert, who led the ill-fated voyage to St. John's Newfoundland. Thus, Sir Walter Ralegh and the famous Gilberts were half-brothers. Katherine brought courtly connections to the Ralegh family. Her brother was Vice-Admiral of Devon and her sister had been Princess Elizabeth's governess before Elizabeth became Queen.

At age fifteen, Walter Ralegh joined a company of English cavalry fighting in France on the side of the Huguenots in the Wars of Religion. He barely escaped the massacre on St. Bartholomew's Day. He had also witnessed the Huguenots' furious murder of French Catholics in Languedoc. That was perhaps his earliest exposure to the horrors of sectarian war.

When he returned from France, Walter attended Oriel College at Oxford but didn't take a degree there. Instead, he read law at the Middle Temple, in London, where he met many influential people and, eventually, was noticed by Queen Elizabeth. At this time, however, Ralegh's half-brother, Humphrey Gilbert, had the most influence on him. He induced Ralegh to join him in an adventure to North America—one given the blessing of the queen in her six-year patent for exploration and settlement in the New World. Captain Ralegh embarked on the *Falcon*, a small ship of about eighty tons owned by William Hawkins, Sir John's father. A Portuguese mariner named Simon Fernandez piloted that ship. (Ralegh would employ Fernandez later in his attempts to colonize Virginia, with disastrous consequences.) Gilbert commanded the *Anne Archer*. On November 19, 1578, they set sail from Plymouth on Ralegh's first sea adventure. The *Falcon* began to take on water at an alarming rate, but Ralegh pressed on. When a storm rose, Gilbert and his other ships returned to port, but Captain Ralegh sailed on, making it to the Canary Islands where he stopped to replenish their water and wine. He continued south, perhaps as far as Cape Verde before the condition of the *Falcon* convinced him it would be impossible to make it to his intended destination of the West Indies. He was home by May of 1579.

By 1580, Ralegh was back in London and a favorite among Elizabeth's courtiers. He had "...a reputation as a proud, hot-tempered, and imperious man..." He was just the man to help with the difficulties in Ireland. The queen sent him there as a captain of soldiers to help put down the rebellion in Munster.

Ireland had been strategically important to England for centuries. A Catholic country by heritage, Ireland's close proximity to England made it an ideal place for a French, or more recently, a Spanish invasion force to gather. Consequently, Queen Elizabeth's father, Henry VIII, had imposed punitive measures on the Irish to bring them into line. The Protestant Church of England had been established through force as the official religion of Ireland. Also, the king or queen of England automatically ruled over Ireland. Finally, Henry and his heirs had begun to anglicize Ireland by outlawing the Irish language and customs and had started a campaign of English plantations in Ireland. They thought by placing English subjects on the ground as settlers in Ireland they could maintain control.

Under Queen Elizabeth, entire regions of Ireland were intentionally devastated to cause famine among the Irish. She also supported punitive raids by English soldiers that killed off whole villages of men, women and children. Thousands of people died as a result of starvation or the English weapons. Ralegh led English soldiers in one campaign that left 600 Irish men, women and children dead in a place still known as the field of skulls.

When he returned to England, he was a regular at court and became a close confidant of the queen. He accompanied her to her various castles and amused himself, when not in her presence, among the maids of honor. Within three years of his return from Ireland, the queen had given Walter Ralegh numerous presents, including the imposing Durham

House on London's Strand. He was clearly enjoying the good life in London.

But at the same time, he must have had a strong desire to do more with his life. Richard Hakluyt had begun publishing pamphlets advocating English settlement of North America. In his book on the history of voyages to North America, Hakluyt presented unveiled goads to the crown to get on with colonization of America. One such passage follows.

Many voyages have been pretended [tried], *yet hitherto never any thoroughly accomplished by our nation, of exact discovery into the bowels of those main, ample, and vast countries extended infinitely into the north from 30 degrees..., neither hath a right way been taken of planting a Christian habitation and regiment upon the same, as well may appear both by the little we yet do actually possess therein, and by our ignorance of the riches and secrets within those lands, which unto this day we know chiefly by the travel and report of other nations, and most of the French...*

This sort of rhetoric would have stirred Walter Ralegh to action. And when his half-brother, Sir Humphrey Gilbert, failed to return from his voyage to Newfoundland in September of 1583, Ralegh took action. He would have been on the voyage with Gilbert had the queen not forbidden it. She had also advised Sir Humphrey to let someone else go in his place, but he insisted on overseeing the expedition himself.

Ralegh may have felt some sense of guilt that he hadn't been along to look out for his older brother. So he approached the queen with a proposal to take over the North American patent she had granted to

Gilbert six years before. Other legal claims left over from the Gilbert debacle had to be dealt with early in the year, and it was March 16 when Ralegh's patent was drafted. The patent, authorizing discovery and settlement essentially within the same bounds as the Gilbert patent, was issued nine days later for a term of six years. Ralegh had an expedition ready to go in about one month, but again had to leave the exploration to other men. We'll touch on what they found and the subsequent voyages of 1585 and 1587 in the next chapters.

Chapter 4
The Outer Banks and the Native People There

The Outer Banks of North Carolina, the site of the first English settlement, have provided a seasonal or year-round home to people for many thousands of years. When people first came to the eastern coast of the Mid-Atlantic region 12,000 or more years ago, the sea level was about 300 feet lower than its current level and, consequently, the sea shore was considerably

Outer Banks of North Carolina

farther east than the current location of the Outer Banks. The climate at that time "was more like the climate in border regions of Canada today…the area [was] covered in boreal (pine) forests…, fresh water river valleys and wetlands." The sea levels rose dramatically during the next six thousand years and the Atlantic shore crept steadily westward. During this process, the native people developed from primarily bands of nomadic hunters into more settled and sophisticated cultures. As the Outer Banks developed, the climate warmed and the salt water sounds behind them provided a lush habitat for various fish, shell fish, crustaceans and other animals. The native people eventually located settlements and campsites on those barrier islands and the adjacent mainland to take full advantage of the abundant fish and wildlife there. As they domesticated plants, they also began to grow the staple of their diet, maize, on the larger islands and the mainland.

The Outer Banks consist of a series of barrier islands that parallel the North Carolina mainland from Cape Fear all the way to Virginia Beach near the mouth of the Chesapeake Bay—a distance of more than 200 miles. These barrier islands are punctuated by numerous relatively shallow inlets that, over the course of time, have opened, closed and migrated due to the effect of the Atlantic currents on the sand that composes the islands. Consequently, the Outer Banks as we know them today are somewhat different than they were when Europeans first sailed there. In subsequent chapters, the historic names of places associated with the early colonial settlements will be matched with modern place names when known. Roanoke Island, the largest interior island sheltered from the Atlantic by the Outer Banks, takes its name from the Indians living there at the time the English came.

Europeans had called the native people of the Americas Indians since the time of Columbus due to the mistaken belief in early years of the Age of Discovery that they had found a new route to the Orient and India. What the Native Americans called themselves varied widely from region to region depending on their language and culture. In the Mid-Atlantic region where the English would eventually establish their first colony, the coastal Indians were of the Algonquian language group. These Indians held territory that bordered with

Iroquois, Muskogee and Mikasuki who were their competitors and trading partners.

Anthropologists refer to the Indians living at the time of European contact as the Woodland Culture. They had highly developed social structures with sophisticated languages, competent counting and arithmetic abilities, and technologies well-adapted to their environment. Some Indian cultures had written languages although those of the Mid-Atlantic coastal region did not.

A Weroance (Leader) of a Virginia Indian Tribe

They were highly successful in their use of the local resources to provide a comfortable life. Although the Europeans looked upon them as savages, heathens, and technologically unsophis-ticated, the Europeans consistently relied on the Indians to provide them with food to sustain them as they set about seizing the Indians lands and trying to convert them to their Christian religions.

The Indians were slightly taller on the average than Europeans. When born, their skin color was nearly the same as Europeans, but it darkened with their long exposure to the sun, and they used various dyes to further enhance their skin color. Both the men and women liked to adorn their bodies with tattoos. Indian men had little facial hair, and what they had, they typically plucked out. The men wore their hair long on one side of their head pulled into a long fall or braid, with the other side shaved. They often painted their head and neck red, black or a combination of the colors. They wore various ornaments in their pierced ears, perhaps a bird claw or something else of small value for a regular tribesman to, perhaps, a string of pearls for a higher-status Indian. Likewise, Indian women of high status wore long chains of pearls around their necks.

Karen Kupperman, noted authority on the sixteenth and seventeenth century Atlantic world, observed that the Indians maintained a higher standard of personal cleanliness than the English who wore the same clothes for long periods, seldom washed and were infested with lice. When the Indians first met the English they must have found them very confusing: people with the technology to build huge sailing ships, with frightening firepower, steel armor, and a stench that the Indians could smell from a great distance.

In artist John White's pictures of Indians from the Roanoke area, he shows the Indian men wearing their hair decorated with a few bird feathers, chains of beads or pearls around their necks and wide, fringed loincloths made of deerskin around their waists. In back, the loincloths have what appears to be a lion's tail with a tuft of hair at the end. The women are shown wearing a fringed loin cloth that hangs nearly to their knees in front and in back. In some pictures, particularly where Indians are depicted working (fishing, cooking, making canoes) the men wear a more abbreviated loin cloth that appears to be an animal pelt (perhaps muskrat) draped across a cord tied around the waist so that the animal's head hangs down at the bottom.

Some of White's paintings show that the women displayed geometric designs tattooed in bands around their upper arms and calves. None of the Indians are shown wearing shoes or moccasins.

This could be because when White saw them, it was in the mild temperatures of summer on the Outer Banks and in terrain where their feet would not need covering.

The Indians lived in villages, maintaining fishing and hunting campsites on the Outer Banks and near the coastal shores. They moved inland to their permanent villages when the seasons dictated.

The family was the fundamental social unit and numbers of families came together to make up villages under the authority of a leader called a weroance. A typical village had between ten and thirty houses made of arched saplings covered with woven mats or bark. The houses were generally

The Village of Pomeiooc

twice as long as they were wide, typically about thirty feet long, but in some cases much larger.

Numbers of villages came under the authority of a superior leader who held a council composed of the subsidiary weroances and tribal elders. The number of villages paying allegiance to the leader was a measure of his ability to command respect among the loosely aligned villages. Thomas Harriot, who sailed to America for Ralegh, wrote, "the greatest Wiroans that we had dealing with had but eighteene townes in his government, and able to make not above seven or eight hundred fighting men at the most..." Harriot was, of course, unfamiliar with Powhatan who would hold sway over a much larger area and many more villages in the Chesapeake Bay region at the time of the later Jamestown settlement. The Indians of the region surrounding Roanoke Island were aware of a great leader to their north, undoubtedly traded with his people, and shared their Algonquian heritage but were not subservient to him.

Indians lived on a varied diet of wild game that they killed with bows and arrows or trapped in snares, fish that they caught in weirs, shell fish they gathered by hand, and vegetables, herbs, fruits and berries that they gathered wild or cultivated. Their staples were Indian corn or maize, grown quite productively in cultivated fields, and venison from the plentiful deer in the forests of the Mid-Atlantic region. Both could be stored to tide them over during the lean winter months. However, they were not unaffected by the vagaries of the weather. Just as Ralegh's farms suffered from floods in England during the last part of the sixteenth century, in eastern America a mini-ice age caused drought conditions that sorely taxed the Indians' ability to keep themselves properly fed. They extracted sugar from corn stalks and, of course, had sweet fruit and melons as delicacies. They grew tobacco for ceremonial or religious rituals.

Women worked hard, tending the fields, preparing food, caring for children, and making and repairing their houses. Men also worked hard. They hunted, fished, built their boats and weirs, and made their tools, weapons and their own clothes. Men would assist the women with some heavy tasks such as clearing fields. Leadership, however, was not the exclusive domain of Indian men. There were notable examples of Indian women who were weroances of their villages or aggregations of villages. One of the Indians who befriended the English colonists at Roanoke Island was named Manteo. His mother was the head of her tribe that had locations on Croatoan Island and the mainland. Similarly, an Indian woman weroance named Opossunoquonuske met and traded with Captain John Smith in Virginia. Indian women owned property and passed it to their heirs when they died. Also, Algonquian society was matrilineal—that is the right to rule passed through the feminine side of the ruling class. When a weroance died, his son didn't become the tribal leader. Instead, his brother (if he had one) became leader. If no brother, then the succession reverted to the mother's family.

Indians placed their dead leaders in this type of ossuary. Note the idol on the left side of the platform.

The Indians held strong religious beliefs. They had many gods, relating to various aspects of nature, but they also recognized a supreme god depicted as a hare, the creator of life, and also a god of evil, Okie, who brought misfortune to mortals. They believed that all mankind descended from an original pair of humans, and they had a myth of a divine flood that destroyed the wicked. The Indian priests also served as physicians and, similarly, "English ministers often doubled as healers," according to Karen Kupperman. She observed that an Anglican religious service would have seemed just as strange to Indians as their religious ceremonies appeared to the English. Indians believed in an immortal soul that went to a heavenly reward or to torment in hell after death depending on the life one led, and some may have believed in reincarnation.

Indian men had to seek permission from their prospective bride's parents and pay a dowry before they could marry. The couples declared their unions in formal ceremonies in front of the assembled village. Indians married within their social caste, as their society had a hierarchy and people were expected to stay within their respective social circles. Indians generally entered into monogamous marriages, although adultery, homosexuality and prostitution were practiced. Some high born Indians had more than one wife as well as concubines.

While Europeans possessed more advanced weapons than the bows and arrows, wooden clubs and shields used by the Indians, in many respects they lacked the necessary technology to make use of the resources in the New World. Indian canoes were faster and much better adapted to the coastal and interior waterway travel of their environment than the large, heavy and cumbersome boats brought to America by the Europeans. And it should be pointed out that many battles in Europe were being fought with bows and arrows well into the sixteenth century. In fact, firearms were relatively ineffective at that time, and most European battles still depended on close-in combat with lances, axes, swords and bows and arrows. The Indians had some metal which they obtained in trade from mines in the interior of the country, and they had some iron that they had salvaged from Spanish shipwrecks. They were proficient potters, making fired clay vessels for cooking or food service and storage, as well as artistic and religious articles.

Finally, it is naïve to think that the Indians knew nothing of the Europeans when the first two ships in Sir Walter Ralegh's advance expedition arrived at the Outer Banks of present-day North Carolina. They had generations of contact or at least oral history of contact with Europeans. In the north, Portuguese, French and English fisherman came in the hundreds if not thousands to fish the fertile banks off Newfoundland every year starting early in the sixteenth century. Some of those men were left behind intentionally or by shipwrecks and, most likely, were known to the Indians if not assimilated into their tribes. Closer to home, the Spanish had explored the coast at least as far as the Chesapeake Bay—their Bahia de Santa Maria. They had left men there including Jesuit missionaries who attempted to Christianize the Indians near where Williamsburg, Virginia, is today. The Spanish had also lost ships on the treacherous shoals along the Outer Banks, and some crewmen made it to shore alive. The Indians told the English settlers of at least two shipwrecks from which survivors were known to have come ashore onto the Outer Banks. More than likely they ended up living with and being assimilated by the local tribes.

Visitors to the New World reported seeing Indians wearing European-style clothing, sailing European ships, and using tools of brass or iron. These artifacts obviously came from contact with Europeans before the documented trips of the known explorers and settlers. Also, the Indians had every reason to fear and mistrust the English settlers when they arrived, based on knowledge of the Spanish atrocities visited on Indians in the south and southwest. The Indians' trade networks were extensive and to believe that the Indians of North Carolina lived in total ignorance of European contact is probably unfounded.

The lives of the Indians of North America had been affected by Europeans long before permanent colonies were established. Documents reveal that:

...the initial contact with Europeans in the [sixteenth] *century had already devastated the native population. Chief Powhatan reported to the English in Virginia before 1610 that he had seen the death of all of his people three times. He probably was commenting on several outbreaks of deadly communicable European diseases for which the Indians had not built up an immunity. Diseases that are considered 'childhood' diseases today and which generally are not life threatening were deadly for the Indians since they had no previous exposure to build up their immunity.*

The Indians of the Outer Banks of North Carolina would learn very quickly and from bitter experience that the new English settlers could be nearly as brutal as the Spanish had been in the southern regions.

Chapter 5
Reconnoitering the Atlantic Coast

Following the failure of Sir Humphrey Gilbert's attempt at colonization in the north, Walter Ralegh began his campaign to acquire the rights of the Gilbert patent and be the first Englishman to settle lands in the New World. On March 25, 1584 (New Years Day in the old calendar) the queen granted Ralegh a new patent, much like the old one Gilbert had received. It reads in part:

Elizabeth by the grace of God of England, France and Ireland Queene, defender of the faith, &c. To all people to whom these presents shal come, greeting. Know ye that of our especial grace, certaine science, & meere motion, we have given and granted, and by these presents for us, our heires and successors doe give and grant to our trusty and welbeloved servant Walter Ralegh Esquire, and to his heires and assignes forever, free liberty & licence from time to time, and at all times for ever hereafter, to discover, search, finde out, and view such remote, heathen and barbarous lands, countreis, and territories, not actually possessed of any Christian prince, nor inhabited by Christian people...to have, holde, occupy & enjoy to him, his heires and assignes for ever, with all prerogatives, commodities, jurisdictions, royalties, priviledges, franchises and preeminences, thereto or thereabouts both by sea and land... and the saide Walter Ralegh, his heires and assignes... shal goe or travaile thither to inhabite or remaine, there to build and fortifie, at the discretion of the said Walter Ralegh, his heires & assignes...

And further that the said Walter Ralegh his heires and assignes, and every of them, shall have, holde, occupie and enjoy to him, his heires and assignes, and every of them for ever, all the soyle of all such landes, territories, and Countreis, so to be discovered and possessed as aforesayd, and of all such Cities, Castles, Townes, Villages, and places in the same, with the right royalties, franchises, and jurisdictions, as well marine as other within the sayd landes, or Countreis, or the seas thereunto adjoyning, to be had, or used, with full power to dispose thereof, and of every part in fee simple or otherwise, according to the order of the lawes of England

The queen's patent also gave Ralegh and those acting on his behalf broad powers to repel anyone of any country who attempted to encroach on the territory he claimed, and gave him and his agents police and judicial powers over the inhabitants of his lands so that they could keep the peace, enforce the laws and could carry out death sentences when warranted under the laws of England. In exchange, the crown would receive "the fift part of all the oare of golde and silver, that from time to time, and at all times after such discoverie subduing and possessing, shall be there gotten and obtained."

The patent presumed that no other Christian prince—meaning the Spanish, French, or Portuguese—had any legitimate claim on the nearly 2,000 miles of coastline from Spanish-held Florida up to Canada. The Spanish and the French would, of course, have felt differently about that. And much more importantly, the Indians already occupied the land and had done so for many millennia, but, since they were considered heathens

50

(that is not Christians), the patent allowed Ralegh to sweep them aside with no consideration for their prior claims on the land.

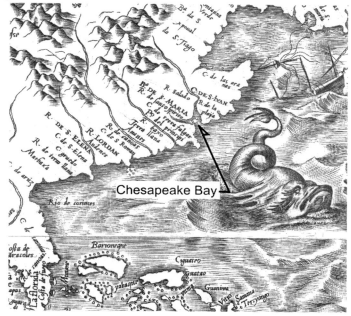

Detail from Spanish Map of 1562.
Bahia de S. Maria is the Chesapeake Bay.

As far as Spanish or French claims on the northernmost part of the continent were concerned, England had a stronger position. According to historian David Quinn, "Englishmen may have sighted Newfoundland as early as the 1480s, and John Cabot clearly delineated eastern Newfoundland, which he thought was Asia, in 1497." Quinn also noted that the English started the cod fishing industry there in 1502, and the other countries followed them there. So, among Christian countries, England had some valid reasons to challenge Spain and France in settlement of North

America, but the Indians clearly had the best and longest-standing claim on the land.

As to the area where Ralegh sent his men, Quinn observes that:

> *In 1566 a Spanish expedition formally annexed the Outer Banks, and thereby North Carolina, to Spain; in 1570 another attempted to found a mission on Chesapeake Bay, but their ships returned only to kill the Powhatan Indians who themselves massacred the Spanish Missionaries.*

Consequently, England's claim on the Outer Banks and the Chesapeake Bay regions was tenuous at best—about as sound as Drake's claim of the Pacific Coast for Queen Elizabeth. The main point is that Spain had not established a permanent presence in the Mid-Atlantic region. Their settlement at St. Augustine in Florida was as far up the coast as they had settled. But it was clear that Spain had a continuing interest in settling as far as the Chesapeake—they just hadn't accomplished it as of 1584.

Ralegh wasted no time in taking advantage of his patent. In April, he dispatched two ships to sail to the New World by way of the established route to the Canaries, across to the West Indies and then up the coast of North America to look for a suitable place to establish his first settlement. These ships were on a mission to reconnoiter and report back on what they had found rather than to attempt to establish a colonial outpost. While they were gone, Ralegh commissioned Richard Hakluyt to write an essay on the importance for England to establish a colony in North America. Hakluyt outlined those ideas in his *Discourse of Western Planting*, which he published in 1584. The essay ran on for 21 chapters, but we can distill from it a number of important points that Hakluyt made:

- An English outpost in North America would be an ideal spot to launch attacks on Spanish interests in the Caribbean and Newfoundland.
- It would prevent Spain or France from taking possession of the land.
- Populating the new land with idle people in England would get them off the charity of the churches and put them to productive work.
- The commodities of the New World would become available.
- The Protestant Religion would be brought to the heathen savages (as the Europeans viewed the Indians)—clearly a goal prompted by fears of the Roman Catholicism the Spaniards forced on the Indians in the West Indies.
- An English outpost would weaken Spain's hold on the West Indies and show the rest of the world that King Philip was no better than the other Christian princes.

In addition, Hakluyt attempted to show that the Spanish Pope's blessing of the 1494 Treaty between Spain and Portugal didn't pose an impediment to England's claim on the North American territory. Hakluyt apparently finished this lengthy essay while Ralegh's ships were on their voyage of discovery, but Ralegh didn't provide it to Queen Elizabeth until the first ship had safely returned to England.

Ralegh had dispatched two men in whom he had full confidence to make that first voyage for him. Philip Amadas came from a similar background as Ralegh and his family lived in Plymouth. Small in stature, he shared another Ralegh trait—his hot temper. Amadas was twenty years old when he commanded this important expedition for Ralegh.

The second leader of the expedition, Arthur Barlowe, had served under Ralegh in Ireland four years before. Both men had some military background but probably not a great deal of seafaring experience. They were accompanied by Simon Fernandez who had served Ralegh as his pilot on his first sea venture aboard the *Falcon* six years before and had sailed *Squirrel* to America in 1580 for Gilbert.

These men and about three dozen more set sail on two well-armed and well-provisioned barks of unknown names on April 27, 1584 from the "west of England," undoubtedly Plymouth. The ships were probably *Bark Ralegh* of 200 tons and *Dorothy*, a pinnace of fifty tons. Both ships belonged to Walter Ralegh. They sailed together down the western coast of Europe and along North Africa, arriving at the Canary Islands May 10th. By June 10th, they had crossed the Atlantic and were on the south coast of Puerto Rico, where some of the men fell sick.

They hurried out of the Caribbean and made good progress up the coast of North America, arriving at Cape Fear in early July. The fragrant scent of pine and magnolia, mingled with the aroma of cooking fires carried on the breezes from the southwest drew them toward the shore. They sailed farther up the coast, keeping the Outer Banks in view and obtaining geographic information that would allow them to return to the coast of present-day North Carolina on subsequent voyages.

Barlowe kept a detailed journal of what they saw and experienced during their time there. As they sailed along, taking soundings of the water's depth and carefully avoiding the shoals, they looked for convenient passages through the barrier islands into the sounds beyond. They finally found a passage near present-day Nags Head, and they named the spot Port Ferdinando (on Bodie Island) after their pilot Fernandez. They went through the passage around July 5th

> ...and after thanks given to God for our safe arrival thither, we manned our boats, and went to view the land next adjoining, and to take possession of the same in the right of the Queen's most excellent Majesty, as rightful queen, and princess of the same, and after delivered the same over to your [Ralegh's] use, ...

They soon found they had landed on an island about six-miles wide and twenty-miles long. They would learn that the Indians called the island Hattorask. As Gilbert had done in Newfoundland, they erected a post with the queen's arms attached to give notice that this land now belonged to England.

After the ceremonies, the men got down to the purpose of the expedition: exploration and documentation of what they found. Three days later, they saw their first Indians in that part of the world. Three men in a canoe paddled into Pamlico Sound and one went ashore near the tip of Hattorask Island. The English were aboard their ships at anchor and watched the Indian walking up and down the beach, looking expectantly at the ships. Finally, Amadas, Fernandez and Barlowe rowed ashore in one of the ship's boats and approached the Indian, who showed no sign of fear of them. The Indian spoke and gestured to the Englishmen, but they couldn't understand what he said. However, they were able to communicate that he was welcome to come aboard their ship and induced him to climb into their boat.

Back on their ship, the English

...gave him a shirt, a hat and some other things, and made him taste of our wine and our meat, which he liked very well; and, after having viewed both barks, he departed, and went to his own boat again, which he had left in a little cove or creek adjoining. As soon as he was two bow-shot into the water he fell to fishing, and in less than half-an-hour he had laden his boat as deep as it could swim, with which he came again to the point of the land, and there he divided his fish into two parts,

pointing one part to the ship and the other to the Pinnace. Which, after he had, as much as he might, requited the former benefits received, departed out of our sight.

Then, about forty Indians came; chief among them was Granganimeo, the brother of the local tribal chief who was named Wingina. Barlowe recorded that they called this country of theirs Wingandacoa. But that was in error. According to Charles Norman, "Wingandacoa" meant "What pretty clothes you are wearing" in Algonquian. This unfortunate error could have left the country with that humorous name, but fortunately Ralegh later selected a politically correct and much more marketable name for the place: Virginia.

The English met with, entertained and traded with Granganimeo and his companions for a number of days, exchanging tin plates and other things of little value for food, furs and pearls. The Indians greatly desired to obtain armor and weapons from the English, but the English resisted, primarily to determine the source of the Indians' pearls, which they highly prized. The English heard of two shipwrecks on the Outer Banks—one about 1558 and the other about 1564. The Indians had salvaged iron from one of the wrecks to make tools. The earliest wreck could have been French or Spanish, but the later one would have clearly been Spanish. Survivors from the earlier wreck had lived for a while under the protection of the Indians and then died in an attempt to sail away in makeshift boats.

In short order, Barlowe felt secure enough to leave Hattorask Island and take a boat across the sound to the northern end of Roanoke Island, where he visited Granganimeo's palisaded summer village—a small encampment of nine houses.

Granganimeo was not home, but his wife greeted the eight Englishmen warmly, even having Indians carry the men from their boat so they would not get their feet wet. They took off the Englishmen's clothes and washed and dried them—a gesture the English took to be one of respect. But more likely the Indians didn't want the unkempt Englishmen to bring dirt and lice into their home. Once the English were suitably presentable, the Indians made a great feast of corn, venison, squash, fish and fruit for them in Granganimeo's house. At this time, they looked upon the English visitors as equals and valued trading partners.

According to Karen Kupperman, the English had a similar perspective of the Indians. She wrote,

When English venturers looked at America's natives they assumed they were looking at people who came from a common stock with themselves. English colonists in the first period of settlement saw the Indians as well within the sphere of normal human beings.

Later, racial prejudice would come to the surface, but at this point the English viewed the Indians as highly competent, although technologically somewhat behind Europe, and merely lacking in an understanding of the Christian (Protestant) religion, which the English planned to remedy as soon as practical.

In the succeeding days, Barlowe continued by boat to explore the sounds from the western side and made note of the villages he was told about or observed. In his travels, Barlowe managed to coax two Indians, Manteo and Wanchese, to sail to England with them. Barlowe's ship, the *Dorothy,* was the first to sail for England about one month after making landfall at the Outer Banks. He made a direct crossing to England arriving with Manteo and Wanchese by mid-September. A small sailboat or pinnace they had assembled at the Outer Banks continued exploring the interior waterways for a short while. Then, Amadas took the bark up the coast to the Chesapeake Bay where the Indians may have been more hostile. As had been the custom on previous voyages and would continue in subsequent voyages, Amadas, perhaps goaded by Fernandez, sailed the *Bark Ralegh* first to Bermuda in hopes of jumping a straggling Spanish treasure ship, and, finding none, continued on to the Azores with similar lack of success. He returned to England a month after Barlowe.

For some time Ralegh had in his household a true renaissance man by the name of Thomas Harriot, a mathematician, alchemist, geographer—in short a scientist—who instructed Ralegh, Amadas and Barlowe in his newly developed application of mathematics to the art of navigation at sea. Harriot's innate curiosity about all aspects of the natural world made him an ideal candidate to examine and document the attributes of the people, the environment, and the commodities of the New World.

Harriot had studied at Oxford where he met Richard Hakluyt, who may have recommended him to Ralegh. Harriot, with his keen interest in languages, had the best opportunity to graduate beyond gestures and sign language and begin to learn some Algonquian words from the Indians newly arrived in London. Similarly, he would have taught Manteo and Wanchese English as fast as they could master it. Harriot spent considerable time working with Manteo and Wanchese in the first attempt to document and translate the Algonquian language—a task for which he developed a unique phonetic system.

Thomas Harriot

It was in both the English and Indian's interests to overcome the language barrier as soon as possible to avoid a simple misunderstanding escalating into warfare. However, Karen Kupperman indicated that the Indians taught the English an abbreviated version of their rich and sophisticated language, a kind of "pidgin," which enabled them to converse with the English but still be able to talk among themselves without fear that the English would understand what they wanted to keep secret. She wrote that they intended to give the English only enough Indian language to facilitate trade.

Once in England, Barlowe and Amadas collaborated on a report for Walter Ralegh that Hakluyt and Ralegh may have edited before distributing it in court circles. In any case, Barlowe wrote a glowing report of the splendor of Roanoke Island. He extolled the virtues of the sixteen-mile-long island as a spot on which to plant the first settlement, but he oversold the fertility of the soil and the capacity of the island to accommodate the hundreds of settlers anticipated to go there.

By November, the explorers and the two Indians had told Ralegh about the many Indian villages and their location within his new territory. They talked about the locations of the principal Indian villages and the rulers they had met in Virginia. Ralegh now had a sense of the immediate vicinity of Roanoke Island. Too bad he had such a poor understanding of how Roanoke Island fit into the big picture that was North America. Unfortunately, Ralegh still didn't understand how inappropriate Roanoke Island and the immediate area around it were for extensive colonization. Even the idea of its serving as a military outpost to support raids on the Spanish was misguided given the shallowness of the entrances to the sound, the difficulty for ocean-going ships to maneuver in the sounds, and the unsuitability of the anchorages off shore in the high winds and crashing seas that plague the Outer Banks at certain times of the year. He would learn this hard lesson at the expense of ships and men in the next phase of the Roanoke Island adventure.

On January 6, 1585, Queen Elizabeth honored Walter Ralegh by conferring knighthood on him for his many services to England including his most recent conquest (vicarious perhaps) of the New World. For his part he deftly cleared up Barlowe's mistaken name for the new territory by asking the queen to let him name their new English territory Virginia in her honor—she was known as the Virgin Queen, having turned down many marriage proposals from the royal houses of Europe including France and Spain. She agreed to the new name and the entire territory from the Spanish outpost at St. Augustine to Cape Breton in Canada became the new English land of Virginia.

In concept, Virginia extended westward to the South Sea, as the Pacific Ocean was known. The English hadn't a clue how big a territory they had just annexed from Spain's North America. And they still hoped to find a short passage across the land, hopefully via water, to Japan, China and India. Others certainly knew better by this time. Abraham Ortelius of Antwerp had published his *Theatrum Orbis Terrarum,* an atlas of the world, about eight years before Gilbert received the first English patent for land in North America. Ortelius's map of North America, apparently based on information compiled by Spanish pilots, overstated the breadth of the continent, but made it clear how great a distance the English would need to cross before they would reach the Pacific Ocean; then they would still have a long sea voyage to reach the orient.

The English apparently did not credit the accuracy of Ortelius's maps, at least with regard to the Northwest Passage. Ortelius's map did not show the deep bay that the Verrazano map had erroneously depicted. Well into the seventeenth century, English maps still showed Drake's land of New Albion on the west coast of North America but a few days journey on foot from the headwaters of the rivers of the eastern seaboard. Certainly, the Spanish knew better.

With the Spanish complaining bitterly to Queen Elizabeth about English interference in the West Indies and North America, Ralegh made plans for his first colonial plantation in Virginia, and the queen had her officials feign ignorance of what Ralegh and his associates had planned. Fortunately for them, Spain was too embroiled in her own problems to mount an effective deterrent to the next wave of English colonists. But, as we'll see, nature and the Indians, as well as lack of focus on the part of the English adventurers, would pose an

insurmountable hurdle for the next English venture
into Virginia.

Chapter 6
The First Colonists Sail for Roanoke Island

When Queen Elizabeth refused to let him lead the next voyage, Sir Walter Ralegh asked Sir Richard Grenville to take his place. Ralegh's cousin from Devon, Grenville had come from a wealthier family. His mother had married Thomas Arundel after her first husband, Richard's father, had died in the sinking of the *Mary Rose*, Henry VIII's huge warship. The Arundels were another prominent family in Cornwall and Wiltshire.

Sir Richard Grenville

Before he was twenty-one years old, Grenville had killed a man in a duel in London. Later he read law at the Middle Temple, joined the army of the Holy Roman Empire and fought the Turks in Hungary. Grenville had come to the queen's notice as Sheriff of Cornwall where he rounded up Catholics suspected of plotting against her. He received a knighthood for these efforts.

Grenville had vied for the opportunity to lead Elizabeth's fleet around the world, but Francis Drake won the honor and profited greatly from the Spanish treasures he seized. Drake used some of his new-found wealth to buy the Grenville home, *Buckland Abbey*, and this may have stimulated in Grenville a strong desire to try his hand as a privateer.

After the return of Amadas and Barlowe in the fall of 1584, Ralegh had worked hard to prepare his plan and the men who would carry it out. In addition to the practical training that the leaders of the expedition received at his expense, Ralegh conferred with various people to get their advice. He didn't want to make the same mistakes that Gilbert had in his attempt to settle in Newfoundland.

He made sure that he had strong political and financial backers, some of whom held the highest positions in Queen Elizabeth's government. One military expert with whom Ralegh consulted advised him to start with 800 well-armed soldiers. Such a force would provide the fortifications and security for the families of farmers, miners and artisans who would follow later. This adviser also recommended engineers, geographers, surgeons, apothecaries and competent artists or draftsmen be included to undertake the necessary studies of the new country's potential for exporting commodities such as minerals, timber, and medicinal herbs, and to properly document what existed there.

According to David Quinn, Ralegh was told to ensure that the soldiers be given orders "that no Indian be forced to labor unwillingly." This seems surprising since the English had no problem engaging in slave trading. They apparently made a distinction between Africans and Indians. In contrast to the advice not to abuse the Indians, Richard Hakluyt wrote that

> ...we will proceed with extremity, conquer, fortify and plant in soils most sweet, most pleasant, most strong and most fertile, and in the end bring them [the Indians] all in subjection and to civility.

That statement seems to be more representative of the English approach to the natives of the New World, considering their punitive approach to the natives of Ireland who were, after all, fellow English subjects.

Ralegh looked to Thomas Harriot to fulfill the role of scientist on the first settlement expedition to America. Along with Harriot, Ralegh arranged for a London painter named John White to accompany the men and document their findings. White, descended from a family in Cornwall, was a member of the London painters' guild. He had sailed with Martin Frobisher in 1577 on a voyage to discover gold in the northern latitudes, and he had painted pictures of Eskimos in the North American Arctic. His accurate sketches not only of the Eskimos but also of their kayaks and domestic scenes showed that he had the talent to document the life of the Indians they expected to encounter in the mid-latitudes of North America. He and Harriot would be responsible for the careful examination of the coastal areas and the accurate documentation of what they would find there.

They would join about 300 men who would be led by Colonel Ralph Lane, a veteran soldier who had fought in Ireland. He would be responsible for the soldiers and would serve as Governor once they were safely delivered to Virginia. Manteo and Wanchese would sail home to Virginia on this voyage. The plan anticipated that an additional 200 settlers would leave two months later to join the colony in Virginia. These settlers would be transported by Amias Preston and Bernard Drake— a cousin of Sir Francis. Drake and Preston had a fleet of three capable ships: the 110-ton *Golden*

Royal, the *Good Companion,* and the seventy-ton *Job.*

Ralegh's settlement was strictly a private venture, although the queen provided a large quantity of gunpowder and one ship, a galleass called *Tiger.* The colonists and soldiers were, for the most part, paid employees of Sir Walter Ralegh rather than adventurers who were paying their own way or going as indentured servants as later Virginia colonists did. The main duties of these first settlers were: to establish a secure outpost; to experiment with agricultural crops; and to conduct more extensive exploration of the region. They would also trade with the Indians to accumulate goods that would be marketable back in England.

One such marketable product that grew in profusion in North America was sassafras, a shrub highly sought for its reputed medicinal benefit in treating venereal disease—a rampant affliction in London at that time. Cedar and other timber would also be worthwhile materials for export to England. And, of course, pearls, furs and skins that the Indians had in large quantities would be highly prized. But the commodity most sought after was the one that had made Spain wealthy—gold. And if not gold, surely silver or copper could be found in abundance, or so the hopeful investors thought. However, the most likely way Virginia would produce gold for the investors would be if one of their ships could snare a Spanish treasure ship during the passage to or from the new colony.

Sir Richard Grenville's flagship was the 160-ton *Tiger*, so it was designated the admiral. Simon Fernandez sailed on *Tiger* as the ship's master and pilot of the expedition. Philip Amadas and Ralph

Lane also sailed on Grenville's ship. Captain John Clarke, one of Ralegh's veteran mariners, commanded *Roebuck*, a medium-sized Dutch flyboat—broad cargo vessel—of 140 tons. Captain George Raymond commanded *Red Lion*, a ship of 100 tons. Thomas Cavendish commanded *Elizabeth*, a small ship of fifty tons that he owned. Ralegh's ship, *Dorothy*, a pinnace of fifty tons was possibly commanded by Arthur Barlowe, according to David Quinn. In addition to these five ships, two small unnamed pinnaces sailed with the fleet.

The typical route to and from America

Approximately 600 men sailed out of Plymouth on April 9, 1585—right on schedule. The ships were fully equipped for the 300 colonists with about one year's supply of provisions, including medicines, meat and fish, tools and fasteners for house building, blacksmith equipment, and the normal military equipment of the soldiers—such things as clothing, pistols, muskets, swords and bows and arrows, as well as armor.

This fleet had a quiet crossing to the Iberian Peninsula where they encountered a fierce storm that sank one of the pinnaces and dispersed the fleet. Grenville and all the commanders of the venture continued on alone in *Tiger* to the Canaries and then to their West Indies landfall at the island of Dominica on May 7th. By prior arrangement, the fleet had planned to regroup at Puerto Rico in the likely event that they had become separated, so *Tiger* proceeded to Guayanilla Bay near the southwest tip of the island. While there, Grenville had the ship's carpenters build a replacement pinnace from locally obtained timber. By May 19th, only *Elizabeth* had arrived. The other three ships had apparently decided to bypass the rendezvous point at Puerto Rico. Some of them may have been cruising the West Indies looking for Spanish prizes to take.

Grenville finally gave up on the other ships and, before leaving Puerto Rico, tried to trade with the Spaniards for supplies. Because the Spaniards seemed more interested in fighting than trading, he left and, sailing through the passage between Puerto Rico and Hispaniola, he captured two Spanish ships. He now knew what it felt like to be a privateer at sea. The small fleet of *Tiger, Elizabeth* and the two Spanish ships set sail for Hispaniola on May 29th, and Grenville ransomed there the Spaniards captured on the two prize ships. Then he bought livestock, taking onboard horses, cows, pigs and sheep for the new colony. He also purchased other cargo including hides, sugar, ginger, pearls and tobacco for transport back to England to help cover the cost of their voyage. He also collected tropical plants at Hispaniola, mistakenly thinking that they would grow in the climate of Virginia.

Chapter 7
Arrival at Their New Home

On June 7th, Grenville gave the order to sail for Virginia. The Spaniards knew that Grenville's mission was to build an outpost in North America but they didn't know where. Indians in Florida gave them some clues when they saw Grenville's ships sailing past St. Augustine. The fleet reached either Cape Fear or Cape Lookout (just north of the present North Carolina-South Carolina border) by June 23rd and veered to the east to avoid the shoals that Amadas and Barlowe had found along the barrier islands in that part of Virginia (now North Carolina).

They reached Wococon (part of present-day Portsmouth and Ocracoke Island) and entered an inlet where the deep-draft *Tiger* soon ran aground. Simon Fernandez took the blame, and they all waited for two anxious hours before the ship floated off the shoal only to run up onto the shore. Much of their provisions were spoiled in the salt water as they unloaded the ship. However, the *Tiger* was not irreparably damaged. In spite of this rough start, they were safely in Virginia. After a couple of weeks spent making repairs, they were ready to begin the next phase of the expedition: establishing a permanent settlement at Roanoke Island sixty miles to the north at the end of Pamlico Sound.

Grenville learned that *Roebuck* and *Dorothy* were farther up the Outer Banks at Port Ferdinando, which he might have wanted to rename after Fernandez (Ferdinando) had run the flagship aground. He sent John Arundel, his half-brother, with Manteo to meet with Wingina, the leader of the Indians there, to discuss landing their settlers on his island called Roanoke. The meeting took place at Wingina's mainland village of Dasemunkepeuc, now the village of Mann's Harbor in Dare County.

A chief of the Roanoke, possibly Wingina

Grenville was shocked to learn that two men from the *Red Lion* were found ashore at Croatoan (Hatteras Island), Manteo's home. They said that Captain Raymond had dumped about thirty men ashore and then sailed off to Newfoundland for a little privateering among the fishing fleet there. So much for their commitment to the mission of planting the first English colony in North America.

Faced with this turn of events, Grenville, Captain Clarke of the cargo ship *Roebuck* and the other ships' captains met to reassess their plans. They had lost one ship, but they still had the two Spanish ships Grenville had captured. David Quinn estimated that they had about 500 men at their disposal, including the ships' crews. He also assumed that some of the livestock would have been lost by this time. Once they saw Roanoke Island themselves, they probably realized that it would not support much more than 100 colonists, so more than half of them would need to be transported home. Interestingly, that number is nearly the same as the first planting of colonists at Jamestown Island twenty-two years later. Of course, Grenville and Clarke expected that a re-supply of men and supplies would arrive in a couple of months when Preston's and Drake's ships arrived. That had probably been the agreed upon plan when Grenville's fleet left England in April. They couldn't know that the plan had changed drastically.

Grenville had a temper, and had already directed it at Simon Fernandez when the ship ran aground. This issue continued to keep the leaders of the expedition agitated, and when Ralph Lane defended the Portuguese pilot, Grenville turned on Lane and many of the other senior men. Lane said Grenville had "intolerable pride and insatiable ambition." On July 12th, Grenville went off on an exploration of the land beyond Roanoke Island in his tiltboat—an open rowboat with a canvas awning over the stern. John Arundel went with him. They were accompanied by Ralph Lane, Thomas Cavendish, Thomas Harriot, Philip Amadas, John Clarke, Francis Brooke, John White, and about thirty other men who traveled in three other boats. This was the first documented exploration of Pamlico Sound. Manteo, Wanchese, or Amadas probably guided them.

The next day, they entered the Pamlico River and went up the Pungo River branch to the Indian village of Aquascogoc (near Scranton in Hyde County). Here a relatively minor incident became a major turning point in Anglo-Indian relations. While they were at the village, an Indian stole a silver cup. The English left that village; went back into the main course of the Pamlico River, and traveled to Secotan, another Indian village farther upstream, where they received a warm welcome. Then this little flotilla of small boats went back downstream and may have gone as far south as the Neuse River before returning to Wococon at the southern end of the sound.

But Grenville, apparently still fuming at the effrontery of the Indian who stole the silver cup, ordered Amadas and his men to go back to Aquascogoc and demand the return of the cup. When Amadas got there the village chief couldn't produce the stolen item, but he promised to locate and return it. That wasn't good enough, and the Englishmen set fire to the village, destroying the Indians' corn and their houses. Over the theft of an inconsequential cup, the English had just alienated one of their neighbors. The word would soon spread among the other Indians that these Englishmen could be very unpredictable and uncivilized.

Wingina had given his permission to the English to move onto Roanoke Island by the second week in July, but Grenville didn't begin to move his men to the island until July 21st.

By July 27th, all the ships of the fleet were anchored together off Port Ferdinando. There were the original ships (missing the *Red Lion* that had skipped off to Newfoundland for some piracy) plus two pinnaces and the two captured Spanish ships— a total of eight ships at anchor. Two days later, the English began transferring their goods ashore, ferrying them through the passage and across the sound to the north end of the island, near Wingina's summer village.

John White's drawing of Roanoke Island and the Outer Banks. North is to the right on this drawing and White's other maps.

While most of the company were clearing land and establishing their settlement, Philip Amadas and one or both of the Indian guides explored the area called Weapemeoc that lay to the northwest of Roanoke Island along Albemarle Sound (the Indians living there were also called Weapemeoc). White and Harriot probably took part in this expedition. The English may also have taken part in a raid by Wingina on a neighboring tribe in which about twenty Indians were killed and women were kidnapped and brought back to Wingina's village. The source for this is an account by an Irishman named Richard Butler whom the Spanish had captured and interrogated. Butler claimed to have taken part in the voyage to Virginia with Grenville.

On August 5th, Grenville sent John Arundel, perhaps the man he most trusted, back in either the

Dorothy, or one of the two Spanish prize ships to take word to Ralegh that they had landed and begun the process of settling in. Arundel had arrived in England by October 14th. On that date, Queen Elizabeth conferred knighthood on John Arundel—the first of her Virginia Knights. Presumably, Arundel told Ralegh—undoubtedly in private—that their mutual relative, Sir Richard Grenville, had been rather heavy handed with the other officers of the colony and with the Indians.

Back at Roanoke Island, Ralph Lane and Philip Amadas saw to the construction of houses and fortifications for their settlement to protect them from Spaniards and the Indians. The defenses consisted of an encircling trench and embankment with bastions projecting from three sides, perhaps with firing platforms at the corners of the enclosure, and cannons mounted on heavy wooden platforms. A small guardhouse completed the fortification. Quinn supposed that they also built houses for the more important members of the settlement (wooden framed with thatched roofs), cottages for the workers, and barracks for the soldiers. Other buildings and structures served industrial purposes such as blacksmithing, metallurgy, and sawing lumber. Also, they had to build communal cooking facilities and latrines. Work on this first settlement had gotten off to a good start once they came to the island, and they made some progress. But the seeds of discontent had been planted, and the gentlemen among the colonists began to complain about their living conditions.

Some vessels left soon after John Arundel, and Grenville set sail on August 25th, leaving behind Ralph Lane as governor of a colony of 107 men. Grenville sailed on *Tiger* and, undoubtedly breathing a sigh of relief, he headed several hundred miles east and nearly four degrees of latitude south to Bermuda, a favorite haunt of the privateers. He was soon rewarded when he captured the 300- to 400-ton *Santa Maria de San Vicente.* He put an English crew aboard, and before the two ships reached Plymouth, he transferred to the Spanish ship, nearly drowning in the process, so that he could have the privilege of bringing her into the English port himself. Although his haul from this bit of piracy fell far short of Sir Francis Drake's record prize, he must have felt somewhat vindicated—the value of the ship and its cargo exceeded what the investors had put into this first colonial adventure. Grenville's success served to reinforce the English idea that serious exploration and colonization could be compatibly combined with piracy or, as they would call it, privateering.

Roebuck sailed from Virginia on or about September 8th with a letter from Ralph Lane bearing that date. He had written to Sir Francis Walsingham, Queen Elizabeth's Secretary of State and spymaster, with glowing praise of the fertility and abundant natural resources of Roanoke Island and the surrounding countryside. He characterized the Indians as friendly, bucolic savages celebrating nature's bounty. From all accounts, it appears that Lane discounted Grenville's harsh treatment of the Indians at Aquascogoc.

Lane expected a supply ship from England to arrive by Easter of 1586, but England was in turmoil with rumors of a Spanish invasion force being assembled. A month after Grenville sailed for America, King Philip finally reached his limit with the English pirates. He ordered the seizure of English ships in Spanish harbors and waters in reprisal. Ironically, while men like Drake, Hawkins and Grenville were out raiding Spanish towns and ships, English merchants were sending their ships to buy and sell goods at Spanish ports throughout Europe and the West Indies. Those merchant ships began to encounter resistance and then outright aggression from their Spanish trading partners.

By June, Amias Preston and Bernard Drake, ready to sail with the second phase of the colonists to Virginia, received countermanding orders from the government. They were to sail with all due haste to Newfoundland to warn the Englishmen there not to sail into any Spanish-controlled ports. Queen Elizabeth also countered Philip's aggression by issuing Letters of Marque to as many privateers as she could enlist. This was a great time to be a pirate.

Although Preston and Drake didn't carry out Ralegh's plan, David Quinn believed that Roanoke was better for it. He thought that another couple hundred colonists and soldiers would have overcrowded Roanoke Island. Nonetheless, Ralph Lane and the other settlers wondered what had happened when no other ships arrived by the onset of winter. Those ships should have arrived by September at the latest.

As time wore on, the investors—or adventurers as they were called—among the colonists soon began to doubt the wisdom of their personal investments of funds and their own well being. The Indians had not brought baskets of gold, pearls or precious gems to Roanoke Island in trade for the trinkets the English had to offer. On the other hand, food was reasonably plentiful and they weren't faced with the sickness and starvation that was to plague the Jamestown colony in later years. The Indians had supplied them with enough corn, venison, fish and oysters to augment their own English provisions, so they made it through the first winter without undue hardship. For the common folk among them, including the soldiers, the living conditions were what they were accustomed to. On the other hand, the gentlemen adventurers would have missed the luxuries they enjoyed in their homes in England.

During the cold months, work continued at Roanoke Island with men tending the animals, repairing the buildings and conducting metallurgical assays. Harriot and White kept busy writing their journals, completing sketch maps and drawings, collecting and painting the flora and fauna they found, and sketching and painting the Indians and their villages. They had ranged a hundred miles or more from Roanoke Island, and Harriot claimed that they had found at least one area rich in iron ore. Bits of melted copper found by archaeologists at Roanoke Island indicate that some metallurgical work must have gone on, but the source of the copper is unknown. Clearly, no one could report finding significant quantities of any marketable metals, not even tin.

Late in 1585, Harriot and possibly White led a group of explorers from the settlement, most likely sailing up Albemarle Sound, out one of the inlets and up to Cape Henry where they entered the Chesapeake Bay. They explored Lynnhaven Bay near present-day Norfolk, Virginia, and White's map shows some details of that area of the Chesapeake including the village of the Chesepioc and Skicoak farther up what today is called the Elizabeth River. They found the Chesepioc (Chesapeake) Indians to be friendly and spent some considerable time with them exploring the south side of present-day Hampton Roads. They came to believe that these Indians would welcome them back to establish a settlement there. These explorers had returned to Roanoke Island by spring 1586. The Chesepioc would have an important place in the later history of the Jamestown settlement in the 17th century.

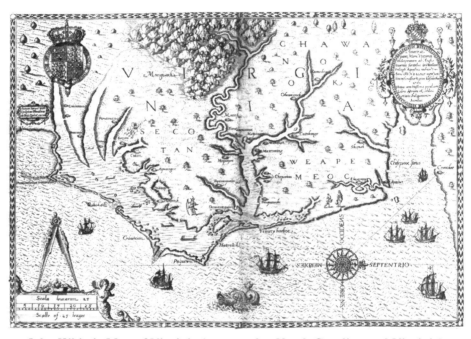

John White's Map of Virginia (present-day North Carolina and Virginia) from the Outer Banks to the Chesapeake Bay published in 1590. Mariners used this map for many years. Note North is to the right.

Chapter 8
Problems Between the Indians and the English

In the spring, Lane had learned a good bit more about the Indians, and what he knew alarmed him. Wingina warned Lane that two tribes on the mainland planned to join forces and attack the English. Whether or not that was true, Lane, being the good soldier that he was, decided a preemptive strike was in order. He rowed up the Chowan River with an armed force, surprised and captured Menatonon, the leader of the Chowan tribe, at his village called Chowanoac (near Harrellsville in Hertford County). But he found no signs that the Indians had assembled an armed force poised to attack Roanoke. With Manteo's or Wanchese's help, Lane interviewed Menatonon and attempted to soothe any hard feelings he had toward the English. Then Lane learned as much as he could about the other Indian tribes with whom Menatonon had contact. He heard about a great Indian leader who lived on a land by a large sea some three days in a canoe and four days march away to the north. That Indian leader, according to David Quinn, may have been Powhatan, or his immediate predecessor. Supposedly, that tribe had had contact with other white men—the Spanish.

Menatonon also told Lane that if he went up the Roanoke River to the land of the Mangoaks (Iroquois), there he would find copper in abundance. Even more copper would be found farther up at a place called Chaunis Temoatan. Lane couldn't wait to go there. Finding copper would silence the gentlemen critics back at Roanoke Island and certainly impress Ralegh and the investors back home in England. As an insurance policy, Lane took one of Menatonon's sons hostage, a boy called Skiko, and he sent him back to Roanoke Island in the pinnace. Lane had two boats, two dogs and about thirty men. They rowed against the current, making slow progress. After three days, Indians attacked them. Although they had no injuries, they were tired and out of food. They had to eat their dogs rather than risk trying to go ashore and hunt deer or other game in the forest. As Lane and his men turned their boats around, the Indians must have had a laugh at the Englishmen drifting down river in their boats, eating dog meat when the woods abounded with game at that time of the year.

They arrived back at Roanoke Island on Easter Sunday or Monday, tired, dejected, hungry, and with nothing to show for their efforts. Lane became convinced that Wingina had caused his problems by turning the other Indian tribes against him. And to add to his misery, the re-supply that had been promised to arrive by Easter was late. He couldn't know it, but it would be months later before the supply ship would arrive, and by then it would be too late to help Lane's settlers. By this time, two expected voyages—one with more settlers and one with supplies—had failed to arrive at Roanoke Island. Anxiety in the settlement continued to increase as a feeling of abandonment set in.

To add to their miseries, Wingina may have been playing a double game, causing unrest among the other Indians while trying to fool the English into thinking he was their friend. At least, that's what Lane came to believe. Lane convinced Wingina to plant corn exclusively for the English and to build fishing weirs for them so that they could catch their own fish, as they had no other means of getting them except from trade with the

Indians. Surprisingly, the English were incapable of building fish weirs themselves even though they had inspected the Indians' weirs.

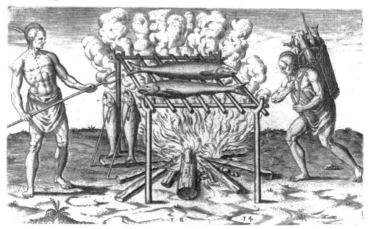

The English depended on the Indians for their food.

Late in April, Wingina's position toward the English changed. His brother, the friendly Granganimeo, had died, and Wingina adopted the new name of Pemisapan. He announced that he was leaving Roanoke Island and was relocating to Dasemunkepeuc, his permanent village on the mainland only a few miles from the island across Croatan Sound. His move may have been innocent enough. The Indians at that time of year needed to get their crops planted and stockpile food to make up for the depletion that always occurred during the winter; but Lane didn't see it that way. He convinced himself that Wingina/Pemisapan had other motives.

In late May, Lane learned that Pemisapan planned to come to the Island in a week or two, feigning friendship, and he and his accomplices would murder the English leaders. Then, according to the rumor, a horde of Indians from neighboring tribes would come in and massacre the rest of the leaderless settlers. Again, ever the bold military strategist, Lane chose the preemptive strike over diplomacy.

Lane, accompanied by Manteo, led a force of about fifty soldiers and executed a night attack on the Indian village at Roanoke on May 31st. The plan called for half the soldiers to capture the canoes so that the Indians couldn't escape, and then to rejoin the force for an attack on the village. In capturing the canoes, Lane's men decapitated two Indians, and others cried out, alerting the village. The Indians in the village took up their bows and arrows when they heard Lane's soldiers coming, and a skirmish broke out in which three or four Indians died in a hail of musket fire. In the morning, Lane's men landed, crossed over to the mainland, and advanced on Dasemunkepeuc, killing many of the leaders. Pemisapan, hit by an English shot, ran into the woods. He was shot a second time in the buttocks as he ran away, but he managed to keep running. Lane ordered soldiers to pursue him and they returned with a trophy for Lane: Pemisapan's head. That ended the skirmish, but began even greater animosity toward the English, thanks to Lane's two military actions against Menatonon and Wingina/Pemisapan. Even Lane must have realized at that point that they could no longer rely on the good graces of the Indians for their sustenance. Lane still held Menatonon's son hostage.

While Lane and the settlers attempted to stay alive at Roanoke in 1585, war was brewing between Spain and England. Preston and Drake had found George Raymond and his *Red Lion* in Newfoundland, and the three of them had a merry time capturing Portuguese fishing vessels. They also managed to jump some Portuguese ships carrying sugar and other goods from Brazil. Portugal was ruled by Philip of Spain at that time and was considered, for all practical purposes, part of Spain, so preying on Portuguese ships was considered a legitimate act of war by the English.

In 1586 at the time Lane was poisoning Anglo-Indian relations, Sir Francis Drake was at his most piratical in the West Indies, greatly irritating the King of Spain. When he sailed in September, 1585, he knew that Ralegh planned to send reinforcements to Roanoke Island, timed to arrive by Easter 1586. So Drake planned to sail there at the end of his punitive cruise through the Caribbean and check on the colonists before returning to England. He started out with about thirty ships at his disposal. Drake had learned that Spain planned to seek and destroy the English colony, and in fact Menendez, the Spaniard who had destroyed the French colony in Florida, was bent on doing just that.

After successfully causing havoc in the West Indies, Drake attacked and destroyed St. Augustine on May 28, 1586, nearly the same time Lane attacked Dasemunkepeuc and killed Wingina/ Pemisapan. Drake had his men strip any useful things from the ruined Spanish fort and then sailed for Roanoke Island. His ships, numbering about thirty-four, were spotted by Captain Edward Stafford at Hatarask Island, and a feeling of relief soon spread through the colony. Drake offered to give Lane

> ...the supply of our necessities to the performance of the action we entered into, and that not only of victuals, munitions and clothing,

but also of barks, pinnaces and boats, they also by him to be victualled, manned and furnished to my contention [satisfaction].

Drake and Lane met on June 11th. Drake was surprised to learn that so few men had been left at Roanoke Island and that the supply ships had not arrived. He hadn't heard what had befallen the Grenville fleet. While Lane felt pressure from some settlers to take the opportunity to abandon the colony and sail for home, he didn't want to give up at that point. He and Drake arrived at a plan where the weakest men could go home with Drake's fleet, and Drake would replace them at Roanoke with some of his own men. He would also leave ships at Lane's disposal on which they could evacuate and relocate to the Chesapeake Bay if that became necessary. Drake designated one his smaller ships, the seventy-ton *Francis*, for that purpose. He also provided two pinnaces and four small boats. And Drake assigned a couple of experienced ship captains to assist Lane. This sounded like a good plan, one which would allow Lane to soldier on rather than creep home in defeat.

In preparation for the trip to the Chesapeake, on June 13th the *Francis* was being loaded, and many of Lane's most trusted men were aboard when a storm struck the Outer Banks. The hurricane lasted three days and pelted the ships and men with hen's egg-sized hailstones. The largest ships put out to sea to avoid being destroyed on the shoals—their anchors couldn't hold against the onslaught of the wind. Many of the pinnaces and small boats were destroyed. Among the ships that put out to sea, the *Francis* had not returned. Lane wanted to continue with the plan in spite of the setback, and Drake offered him the *Bark Bonner* of about 150 tons, but it drew too much water to enter the sound and pick up the passengers. Lane decided the *Bark Bonner* would have a similar disadvantage in the Chesapeake—in that he was wrong since, ships of the Virginia Company of equal size navigated there without difficulty in later years.

Lane finally reached the conclusion on June 17th, with some encouragement, no doubt, from the colonists, that the sane thing to do would be to abandon plans to go to the Chesapeake and, instead, return to England with Drake. From there, things got a bit frantic. Drake's sailors wanted no more of this vulnerable position on the Outer Banks. They brought the longboats to Roanoke Island to ferry the colonists through the inlet at Port Ferdinando and out to the waiting ships, but they had no patience for the settlers' pleas to give them more time to pack their belongings. The sailors forcibly marched the colonists out of the settlement and into the boats, tossing excess baggage into the sound as they rowed for their ships. Many valuable possessions were either left at the settlement for the Indians to find or ended up in the water. That included a string of pearls intended for Queen Elizabeth and, much more important, some of White's maps and Harriot's scientific collection. They left so quickly, in fact, that three men were left behind on the mainland. Those men had been sent by Lane to take Skiko back to his father Menatonon. They were never seen again, and they became the first of the so-called Lost Colonists.

One of the accounts of the storm and the subsequent departure provides a moral tone, blaming the settlers' unfortunate situation on their abuse of the Indians:

...they left all things so confusedly, as if they had bene chased from thence by a mightie armie, and no doubt so they were, for the hande of God came upon them for the crueltie, and outrages committed by some of them against the native inhabitants of that Countrie.

White, Harriot, Lane, Manteo and Towaye (another Indian) boarded Drake's flagship, the 600-ton *Elizabeth Bonaventure*, one of the queen's own ships. They set sail for England by way of Newfoundland on June 18th and made it to Portsmouth on July 28, 1586. Lane was ready to put together another colonial venture and return to America as soon as possible, but that would have to wait. Spanish invasion of England was imminent and Ralegh, already deeply involved in Ireland, couldn't afford to spend any more time on Virginia because of his duties related to the defense of England.

In considering why this first attempt failed, David Quinn said

[the venture's] *bias on the military side emphasized the colony's position as an outpost against Spain, as a possible base for ships operating against Spain, and a possible target for Spanish attack. It also indicates that the colony had to guard against the hostility of the native inhabitants.*

Quinn characterized this first colony as "...primarily an experiment in colonization rather than the first step...for establishing a lasting society of English people across the Atlantic." On the other hand, what emerged was a pragmatic decision by Sir Richard Grenville and the other leaders of the venture to place sufficient men on the shore to hold the position for a follow-on colonial planting with the optimum composition of men, women, supplies and equipment.

It may be too harsh to second guess their decision to leave less than the full complement of men in 1585. In fact, had they left several hundred as originally planned, it's doubtful the outcome would have been any different, and their living conditions might have been less secure, leading perhaps to disease and death during the first winter. Likewise, Drake and Lane correctly assessed the situation at Roanoke Island in the early summer of 1586: the men were demoralized, the Indians could not be counted on for support (a protracted drought most likely meant they had trouble enough feeding themselves), and the colony didn't have the resources they needed to endure another winter without significant Indian help. Perhaps they could have tried again at the Chesapeake Bay location, but the men didn't have the will at that point to start over in a relatively unknown land where they would have to work hard at building houses, fortifications and, most importantly, good diplomatic relations with the Chesapeake Indians. On the balance, their decision to retreat and try again as soon as possible was the correct one.

Chapter 9
Grenville's Return to Roanoke Island

Indians of the Outer Banks observing the comings and goings at Roanoke Island must have wondered what the English were doing. Ships came and went every couple of weeks, taking the original settlers away and leaving none in their place—very confusing.

Ralegh had sent the supply ship for Lane's settlement, but the ship left four months later than expected. This may have been due to the many distractions Ralegh had at the time: impending Spanish invasion, his military duties, his work recruiting settlers for his plantation in Ireland, and various official positions he held such as his responsibility for the Cornish tin mines as Lord Warden of the Stannaries. In any case, the timing was very unfortunate. The supply ship that left England after Easter in 1586 arrived at Roanoke Island in late June, about one week after Drake had sailed away for England with all but three of Lane's settlers. The arrival of the supply ship might have given Lane and his colonists the morale boost they needed to persevere. The supply ship's crew searched the island and found evidence of the storm damage to the settlement. They also saw that the settlement had been abandoned in haste. They must have wondered what could have caused the settlers to leave so abruptly and where they could have gone. But they weren't prepared for a protracted search. They left Roanoke Island as they found it and sailed back to England.

Meanwhile, Sir Richard Grenville, with six ships carrying 400 soldiers and sailors, sailed on April 16, 1586 for America. When they left

England, Lane was still at Roanoke Island, but he would be gone by the time Grenville could get there. Grenville had the queen's authority to take any Spanish prizes he found. Instead, he was an indiscriminate pirate, and he captured one English and two French ships before he left continental waters. He also took a Dutch ship and added it to his fleet, now numbering seven. When he reached the Madeiras, he headed west to make a direct crossing to Virginia. He arrived at Roanoke Island only a week or two after Ralegh's supply ship had departed. He searched for a couple of weeks and found only two bodies, one an Englishman and one an Indian, both of whom had been hanged. David Quinn speculated that the hanged men would have been evidence of some conflict that arose among the crew of Ralegh's supply ship that had been at Roanoke only a matter of weeks before Grenville arrived there.

Grenville learned from a captured Indian who spoke English that Drake had evacuated Lane and his men only a few weeks before. This Indian remained aboard Grenville's ship and eventually became educated in England. He was christened and given the name Ralegh. He died in England and was buried in the churchyard in Bideford, Devon in 1589.

Grenville decided to leave a very small company of men on Roanoke Island to literally hold the fort until another expedition could be prepared and sent to the island. Why he left so few men is puzzling, but considering that he had started his voyage with six ships and only had 400 men, he may have decided he could use them to greater profit in piracy rather than in colonization. In any case, his decision was a bad one. He left fifteen or eighteen men (there are conflicting accounts), and they were clearly too few, even with their somewhat superior arms and armor, to resist any attack by Indians. Obviously they could never have repulsed an attack by Spanish forces, who Grenville had every reason to believe would come looking for the English colony at some point.

When Grenville left Roanoke Island, he directed part of his fleet south to Bermuda and hoped to take another Spanish treasure ship, but found none. The other part of his fleet went north to the fishing banks off Newfoundland to see what ships they could catch there. Grenville continued from Bermuda to the Azores and robbed a local ship and captured another ship with a valuable cargo of sugar, ginger and hides. He was back at Bideford, England by the day after Christmas, 1586.

As to the men left behind at Roanoke Island, a year later these Englishmen had also mysteriously disappeared. The Indians would tell a story about them being attacked by a combined force of warriors from Dasemunkepeuc, Aquascogoc, and Secotan. Those Indians surprised the English outside their fort. One Englishman was killed by a blow to his head from a club. The rest ran to one of their houses where they grabbed whatever weapons they had handy. The Indians flushed them out by setting the thatched roof on fire. The English ran into a hail of arrows, one dying from an arrow shot into his mouth. The rest of the men made it to their boats and rowed across to the outer island. They stayed on the Outer Banks for a while and then disappeared, never to be seen or heard from again. They had suffered the fate that Lane feared would come at some point, and it gives further support for his decision to abandon Roanoke Island. That event added thirteen more missing men to the mystery of the lost English colonists of Roanoke Island. The count now stood at sixteen.

When Lane had returned to England with Drake, Ralegh was busy with his estate at Youghal in Ireland. He had dismissed Lane with the order to write a full report of what had transpired in Virginia. Lane concluded in his report that the territory of Virginia would not be worth further effort unless it yielded gold or silver mines or a passage to the Pacific Ocean. But Ralegh saw another reason for Virginia: it would serve England well at that time of war if they could establish a deep-water port there from which to attack Spanish ships in the Caribbean and Newfoundland. By then he knew that Roanoke Island and the Outer Banks would not be the best location for that port. Instead he turned his attention to the Chesapeake Bay. That appeared to be where he should make his next venture. Meanwhile, at his Irish estate, Ralegh planted potatoes (the first in Ireland) and tobacco that Harriot had brought back on Drake's ship. Ralegh concluded that it was much easier to recruit settlers for agricultural plantations in Ireland, and they could be more profitably managed from the close proximity of England.

However, much had been accomplished during the year of Lane's settlement. David Quinn observed that

> *No area of eastern North America was so thoroughly examined for many a long year as that of Roanoke Island and its hinterland by Thomas Harriot and John White during the period from July 1585 to June 1586, and no*

survey of its kind would be done again until long after the American Revolution.

Harriot eventually published *A brief and True Report of the new found land of Virginia...* with accurate maps and excellent drawings originally produced by John White and engraved for publication by Theodor de Bry. Harriot and White produced much more, but, unfortunately, many of their documents have not survived. Harriot's book would become a manual for the colonists who would later settle permanently at Jamestown in 1607. Because of Harriot and Ralegh, tobacco became an important commodity in England. It had been introduced by seamen in earlier times, but Harriot hooked Ralegh and Ralegh hooked the courtiers in the queen's court, and from there tobacco made it into the pubs and coffee houses throughout England.

Ralegh learned from Harriot that Indian corn or maize was a staple on which the English could depend. However, he failed to grasp how dependent the Indians were on hunting and fishing to augment their agricultural production. When the next waves of colonists went to America, including the Virginia Company's Jamestown colonists in 1607, they would not be properly equipped to take advantage of the wild game and seafood resources, and would continue to be vulnerably dependent on the skills of the Indians for their sustenance and survival.

Chapter 10
The Planting of the Second Colony

Once Grenville had returned at the end of 1586, Ralegh knew that Roanoke Island was not significantly occupied. In fact, it was probably abandoned by then, but he couldn't know that. Ralegh began to assemble ships, men and equipment for another attempt to keep his Virginia patent alive. Recruiting was more difficult this time because some of the gentlemen adventurers who had returned with Lane were telling anyone who would listen what a waste of time Roanoke Island had been and how deplorable the living conditions were in that land among the Indians.

Ralegh still hoped that the Chesapeake Bay could be the fabled passage to the Pacific Ocean, and he set his sights on the Chesapeake for his next colonial attempt. Richard Hakluyt supported this plan. Hakluyt knew that Spaniards had found silver ore at the latitude of about 37 degrees in the west and he suggested that, since the Chesapeake was at the same latitude, silver must be in that region. Hakluyt, of course, didn't realize that there were thousands of miles of unexplored land between the Spanish mines in the southwest and the east coast of America.

Sir Richard Grenville wouldn't take the next group of settlers to Virginia. Like Ralegh, he had his own interests in Ireland, and if he neglected them, he would forfeit his land grants. John White stepped forward to lead the next settlement to the Chesapeake Bay where he expected the Indians to be friendly. Ralegh selected the previously reliable Portuguese pilot, Simon Fernandez, to provide transportation to Virginia. White planned to call at

Roanoke Island to see to the men left there by Grenville and then continue on up the east coast to the Chesapeake Bay where they would find a suitable landing place for their colony on the south side of the present-day James River.

Ralegh knew by now that he would need a more well-balanced complement of settlers. This time he would send artisans, farmers, metallurgists, surgeons, and all the other trades needed to build and operate a thriving village in the New World. He would also send women as well as men. This was to be a permanent establishment, and, as an inducement, he would offer land for those willing to go to Virginia and remain there. He knew that relying solely on the Indians for support would be risky, so these families should have the ability to grow their own food on the land that Ralegh would grant to them. This scheme also had the advantage of getting the settlers off of Ralegh's payroll. Where most of the previous settlers under Lane drew a wage from Ralegh, the new colonists would be given land in lieu of money for their efforts. This proved a good inducement, since most English families living on land owned by the aristocracy, had no hope of owning land in England or Ireland.

Because so many West Country men had staked claims for land in Ireland, recruiting settlers there for America proved difficult. Faced with the prospect of a short sail across the Irish Sea where they would find paid employment on land very similar to that at home, most prospective settlers would take that opportunity instead of the offer of land of their own in a hostile country that could only be reached after starving for several months aboard a cramped and stinking ship, pitching and rolling through hazardous seas patrolled by pirates and Spain, the arch-enemy of England. So Ralegh and John White recruited many of the settlers from the southeast of England and London where unemployment was high and the living conditions were appalling.

Ralegh formed a new organization—the City of Ralegh in Virginia—headed by himself, of course. John White was Ralegh's assistant, but for all intents was responsible for the organization of this new attempt at settlement, according to lebame houston, Elizabethan scholar at Roanoke Island. White would have the title Governor when the settlers arrived in Virginia. Families in Virginia would each receive 500 acres—an unheard of amount of land for most people in England. Investors who remained in England would be paid dividends from the profits Ralegh supposed would accrue from the sale of gold, silver or other commodities exported to England from the colony. Probably some of the settlers arranged for someone else to pay their passage and entered into indentures (contracts) to work for several years to repay their sponsors.

White had twelve assistants, including his son-in-law, Ananias Dare, and Simon Fernandez. Three of his assistants remained in England. All thirteen of these adventurers received grants of arms, instantly making them gentlemen in English society. About 150 settlers were recruited, but not all of them boarded the ships when the time came to sail. About 120 embarked on the voyage, and 115 of them remained on Roanoke Island.

They had three ships: *Lion* of 120 tons, the flagship with John White and Simon Fernandez, Manteo and Towaye aboard; a flyboat of twenty tons with Edward Spicer as master; and a pinnace with Captain Edward Stafford, a veteran of the Lane expedition to the Chesapeake, in charge. On or about April 26, 1587 they departed London for the Isle of Wight and then Plymouth where they remained until May 8, 1587. This was a woefully late start since it would put them in the New World months after their crops should have been planted, and they would arrive in the middle of the hurricane season.

In the overall scheme of things, England and Sir Walter Ralegh had more important things to focus on than White's tiny expedition, and that may explain why it took so long for the settlers to find transportation, load supplies and depart. The defense of the English homeland was of paramount importance, and all English ships would soon be pressed into that campaign. White's little fleet really made it out of England in the nick of time.

Whether Simon Fernandez ever had any interest in this colonization effort is doubtful. David Quinn wrote,

> *...no student of his* [Fernandez'] *personality and actions can believe he was wholly sincere. From the first he may have supported the new venture in hopes of exploiting it for himself as its admiral and without any real intention of helping to make the proposed settlement a permanent one or its interests paramount.*

Quinn supposed that Fernandez might have intentionally delayed their departure from England. Why would he have done so? For the very good reason of timing—had he left earlier, he would have been saddled with White and his colonists through the voyage to the West Indies and have been inhibited in doing what it turned out he most wanted to do: raid Spanish ships. By leaving so late, it would put him in Virginia in late July or early August, which was perfect timing to drop the settlers and get onto the business of snagging Spanish treasure ships as they sailed past the Bermudas on their way to Spain.

Whatever Fernandez' motivation, White soon saw his true colors. Off the coast of Portugal, Fernandez left the flyboat in his wake. They were only eight days at sea at that point, and White watched helplessly as the cargo ship, containing their supplies and equipment, vanished in the distance.

In the West Indies, White and Fernandez disagreed over where to take on supplies, and White expressed his frustration in his diary. Unaccountably, White, throughout his adventures, never proved able to take charge or assert his authority, particularly over Fernandez. This is all the more surprising in that Ralegh, when he sailed with Fernandez, had no trouble controlling him. Likewise, Sir Richard Grenville maintained his authority when Fernandez sailed as his pilot.

In White we see a very talented artist, an empathetic man who saw the humanity of the Indians, but clearly not a man cut out to lead such an expedition. In fairness, Fernandez clearly had the power aboard ship. He had recruited the sailors who expected a share of any prize they captured, and they owed him their loyalty. They wouldn't have listened to the likes of White in any case. So, White bowed to Fernandez every time.

The colonists proved they were not timid passengers while in the West Indies. They went ashore, explored, found water to bring back to the ship, and shot swans for food. They also saw Indians on the Islands but had no contact with them.

Two of the colonists defected and joined the Spaniards in the West Indies, reducing their number to 118.

Fernandez preferred to cruise among the islands and opposed White's suggestions that they go ashore to trade or forage for supplies to take to Virginia. It seems logical that Fernandez wanted to loiter within the Caribbean to try his luck at capturing a valuable cargo to make his voyage worthwhile.

Finally Fernandez departed the Caribbean and sailed up the coast of North America. He anchored the *Lion* and her pinnace off of Port Ferdinando on July 22. White planned to go ashore on Roanoke Island to confer with Grenville's men and then continue on to the Chesapeake Bay, but now Fernandez' real intentions became quite clear. White was told that Fernandez had decided that "...the summer was far spent wherefore he would land all the planters in no other place." In other words, get out now, this is as far as you're going. White accepted this decision, writing in his diary that essentially it would have been no use to argue with Fernandez. Eighty-nine men, seventeen women and nine children went ashore in Virginia to start a new colony at Roanoke Island.

Now the fate of those 115 colonists rested on Manteo's diplomatic skills. White expected to find a dozen or so men on shore (the ones left by Grenville), and a well-maintained fort and settlement to move his settlers into. They could regroup there and then use the pinnace to ferry settlers up to the Chesapeake Bay as time and the weather permitted. To his shock, when he went ashore on Roanoke Island, he found the skeleton of one dead Englishman whitening in the harsh summer sun, the fort leveled and rampant weeds and saplings growing up among the houses. But White bent to the task at hand and directed the colonists to repair the houses and cottages, and presumably to restore the fortifications. He must have bemoaned the loss of the supplies and equipment on the flyboat, but, much to his delight, the cargo ship arrived on July 25th, only three days behind the others. At least he had all the supplies and his settlers at the island.

The settlers would have been nervous at what they found—not at all what they had expected—but they continued to settle in, until George Howe went crabbing. An Indian hunting party stumbled onto him and left him dead with sixteen arrows in his body, his head shattered by an Indian's club. The new colonists now knew that all was not well at Roanoke Island, and they probably rightly concluded that a similar fate had befallen Grenville's men.

White sent Captain Stafford and Manteo to meet with his tribe at Croatoan. When they got there, the Indians feared they had come to seize their corn, which was in short supply. Manteo soon quieted their fear and the village turned out to give them a warm welcome. But the Indians were still nervous about some of the English. They hadn't forgotten that Lane's soldiers had attacked them on the mainland, mistaking them for Wingina's men. They asked the English to give them some emblem to signify their friendship so that they would not be mistaken for the enemy again. Stafford would have been well-advised to do that, but he let it pass. The Croatoan Indians told Stafford that the Indians at Dasemunkepeuc, led by Wanchese after Wingina's death, had killed George Howe, and they blamed

Wanchese in concert with the Indians from Aquascogoc and Secotan for the death of Grenville's men. Alarmed by the story Stafford, convinced the Croatoan Indians to call for a meeting between the Indians of the region and the English at Roanoke Island to try to patch up their differences.

The meeting was scheduled to take place by August 8th. But no Indians came—not even from Croatoan. White decided to take military action against the hostile Indians as Lane had done before. He took Manteo, Captain Stafford and twenty-three men to raid Dasemunkepeuc. White's force crept under cover of darkness into positions surrounding the village. They charged into the enclosure, taking the Indians by surprise and killing one. To their horror, they soon discovered that the Indians were Manteo's own people.

The Croatoans had learned that Wanchese had taken his people into the interior after they had killed George Howe, obviously fearing the English would react with force, and Manteo's people had come to the abandoned village to scavenge whatever had been left behind. Manteo told them that if they had maintained contact with the English after their visit to Croatoan, the killing wouldn't have happened. For their part, the Indians probably reminded Manteo that they had asked for some emblem from the English that they could have worn to prevent just what happened. After much finger pointing, everyone returned to Roanoke Island (Indians included). Manteo and White did what they could to smooth over the hard feelings.

Manteo became a Christian and also received the title of Lord of Roanoke and Dasemunkepeuc on August 13th. Five days later the first English child born on North American soil entered the world. She was the daughter of Elenor White and Ananias Dare. Six days later, she was christened Virginia for obvious reasons. Another child, born a short time later to Dyonis and Margery Harvie, added another much less famous name to the number of the colonists. There's no record of his or her first name, so all school children learn about Virginia Dare, granddaughter of Governor White, but nobody hears about poor (Blank) Harvie. With his/her birth there were 116 settlers at Roanoke Island in 1587.

Chapter 11
The Settlers Become Dispirited

In the time between his granddaughter's birth and christening, John White had to confront a most perplexing problem. The settlers had come to the conclusion that, because they had been put ashore at Roanoke Island instead of the Chesapeake Bay as Ralegh's mission called for, someone they could trust must return to England as soon as possible to alert Ralegh so that supplies would arrive at the correct location. Various people were considered, but, finally, on August 22nd they presented White with the ultimatum that he must go for the well-being of the settlement. They could have chosen him for a number of good reasons: he had demonstrated a singularly poor ability to lead them; he had a daughter and granddaughter who would remain at Roanoke Island and thus give him an excellent reason to return after diligently assembling the needed supplies; and his standing with Sir Walter Ralegh meant he would receive priority during those difficult political times.

White hesitated because he feared his early return to England would be misinterpreted as having abandoned his responsibilities in Virginia, making it harder to recruit more settlers. He also had valuable belongings in Virginia, and he worried about who would protect them from theft or damage. The settlers told him they would keep his belongings secure and gave him a letter stipulating that he had returned at the request of the settlers to see to their welfare. The document made it clear that White reluctantly accepted the settlers' entreaty to return to England on their behalf.

While all these debates raged on, a storm lashed the Outer Banks, forcing the *Lion* to put out to sea to avoid damage on the shoals. She didn't return until August 27th, and might not have returned at all if part of her crew hadn't been left ashore when the storm hit. White made hasty preparations for his voyage and left instructions with the settlers that, when they left the island for a better site, they must leave a message saying where they had gone. If they left in distress, they were to add a cross to the message so that he would know of their danger. The settlers' plan at the time White bid them farewell was to relocate fifty miles into the mainland. David Quinn theorized that their intended destination was the location of the Chesapeake Indians with whom some of Lane's men had spent the winter of 1585/86.

Instead of boarding the *Lion* with Fernandez for the return voyage to England, White ended up on the flyboat around midnight on August 27th. Why he sailed on the cargo ship instead of the flagship on which he had traveled before is an unresolved question. It may be that he didn't want to be that close to Fernandez. It could have been Fernandez' decision—another humiliation of White. As the small number of crewmen on the flyboat manned the capstan to raise the anchor, a shaft broke and the capstan spun out of control, injuring several men in the process. On the second attempt, additional men were injured. Finally, Captain Spicer ordered the anchor cable cut, and they got the cumbersome ship underway. They tried to keep up with Fernandez in the *Lion* as he sped toward the Azores and, he hoped, rich pickings among the Spanish treasure ships.

They came near the Azores after three weeks of sailing, but had precious little drinking water and only five able seamen to man the ship. The next day they left the *Lion* astern and headed north toward England. They sailed on for a few days when they ran into a huge storm that drove them well south into the uncharted Atlantic. The foul weather prevented determining their latitude by the normal observation of the sun and stars. When they finally found favorable weather, they took thirteen days just to regain their position before the storm. They were now truly desperate, the crew sick and out of water. The flyboat struggled into a port on the southwest coast of Ireland where White saw to the safety of the men and the salvage of the ship. Then he found a ship bound for England and made it to Cornwall on November 1, 1587. When he got to Southampton seven days later, he heard that the *Lion* had already arrived in port, having returned with nothing to show for their privateering.

White received more shocking news when he landed. On October 9th, Queen Elizabeth had ordered that no vessels could leave English ports. Ralegh, however, had some discretion at first. Sir Richard Grenville was preparing a relief mission, and Ralegh provided a ship for White to return immediately. By late March, 1588, Grenville had five or six ships loaded and ready to sail, and White had recruited additional settlers who had relocated to Bideford for their departure. They would have made it, but contrary winds kept the ships bottled up in port. Before they could sail, the queen ordered the ships to Plymouth and placed them under the command of Lord Howard of Effingham and Sir Francis Drake. The probability of attack by the Spanish Armada prompted the queen's action.

White had delayed too long, ending any hope to reach the colonists reasonably soon. The upshot of that decision was that 115 settlers joined the growing list of English men, women and children abandoned in Virginia. The count now stood at 131.

But White wouldn't give up. Ralegh arranged passage for White and perhaps a dozen settlers aboard a bark of thirty tons called *Brave*. That ship and a pinnace named *Roe* were not capable of joining the defense fleet and so could leave port. They finally got underway on April 22nd, and Captain Facy and his pilot Pedro Diaz immediately set to, capturing eight ships of various nations. White found himself aboard nothing more than a pirate ship. *Brave* soon left *Roe* behind. Near the Madeiras, a French ship engaged Facy's ship and boarded her. In the ensuing battle with cutlasses, lances, muskets and pistols, White received a sword and lance wound to his head and a shot in his buttock. Three other passengers were wounded. There were many casualties, and Pedro Diaz joined the French pirates. Eventually Diaz landed in Havana and wrote an account of these adventures.

Robbed of everything of value, *Brave* arrived back at Bideford on May 22, 1588. White later wrote that "God justly punishing our former theeverie of our evil disposed mariners." That disastrous voyage proved the end of the line for White. Ralegh and Grenville had no time to talk to him; the Spanish fleet would arrive any day. White would have to wait two years before conditions improved sufficiently to mount another mission to fulfill his promise to the Roanoke Island settlers.

However, had he made it to Roanoke aboard the *Brave,* White might have run into a Spanish expedition searching for the English settlement. According to David Quinn's research, the Spanish governor of Florida sent another search party under Captain Vincente Gonzalez who had experience in the Bajia Madre de Dios del Jacan (as the Spaniards had taken to calling Chesapeake Bay). They made a thorough search of the lower James River, the Potomac River and even sailed as far as the Susquehanna River that flows into the headwaters of the bay. On their return voyage down the coast, they went into the sound near Roanoke Island through one of the inlets from the Atlantic and found evidence that people had been living there, but didn't find the settlers. Quinn estimated that Gonzalez stopped there in June of 1588 since he had returned to St. Augustine by July. So wherever the Roanoke Island settlers had gone, they must have departed the island between late August 1587 and June of 1588.

Chapter 12
White Finds a Message at Roanoke Island

Ralegh had little time for White, but he did set up a syndicate of London investors to help him organize a return voyage to Roanoke Island. The men of the syndicate included William Sanderson, one of Ralegh's business associates, and Thomas Smith. The Smiths were prominent merchants and investors in London, and Thomas Smith would become one of the principals in the Virginia Company that, about fifteen years later, would successfully launch England's first permanent colony in America.

The investors, many of whom were London merchants, received licenses to trade with the City of Ralegh in Virginia. This new syndicate received its royal charter on March 7, 1589. White now had the financial backing to try to reach the colonists, but he couldn't sail in 1589. There were a number of reasons. First, White would not want to make the same mistake he made in sailing with someone as untrustworthy as Captain Facy, the master of the *Brave*; he would be more careful this time. Second, even had he found a reliable privateer, they wouldn't likely have been diverted from their lucrative raiding activity to carry men and supplies to the colony. Third, the royal ban on commercial voyages was still in effect. Fourth, Sir Francis Drake was preparing a massive naval counterattack against Spain by invading Lisbon, Portugal, with a goal of breaking the Spanish hold on that country. Drake's mission absorbed many, but not all of the ships available at that time. White had to wait more agonizing months, frustrated by delay after delay, not knowing how his daughter and granddaughter were faring.

When Ralegh returned to London early in 1590 he found no progress with respect to the relief mission for the Roanoke colonists. Ralegh, White and Hakluyt had different opinions on the best approach. Ralegh favored a combined privateering swing through the Caribbean followed by a call at Roanoke. White wanted to ferry new settlers and supplies directly to Virginia with no distracting piratical sidelines. Hakluyt favored a single-purpose trip taking a direct route across rather than the longer, more dangerous route through the Caribbean. Ralegh left it up to William Sanderson to make the arrangements. Although merchant ships were still banned from sailing, privateers could sail, as had Drake. It became clear that privateering would play some part in White's next voyage as well.

Sanderson found a ship of 80 tons he renamed the *Moonlight.* Captain Edward Spicer, a veteran of the previous voyage, signed on to command her and a forty-man crew. They fitted her out with seven cannon for protection and loaded on the supplies. For additional security through the Caribbean, Ralegh made arrangements for the *Moonlight* to sail in company with a privateering fleet composed of three ships: *Hopewell*, a ship of about 150 tons with at least sixteen guns and a crew of eighty-four commanded by Master Abraham Cocke; *Little John*, a ship of about 120 tons with nineteen guns and about one hundred men under the command of Captain Christopher Newport (a very important man for the Virginia Company in future years); and *John Evangelist*, a pinnace under the command of Captain William Lane. The backer of this privateering venture, John Watts, posted a £5,000 bond to assure Ralegh that he would carry out his duties with respect to the Virginia settlement.

When White came to the Thames dock to board his settlers, Abraham Cocke, master of the *Hopewell,* refused to take any aboard except for White. He told him to either get on alone or stay on the dock and miss the voyage entirely. White later wrote that he had no time to call on Ralegh or Sanderson to change Cocke's mind. Why Cocke took that stand is unclear, but we can speculate that it reflected his emphasis on the privateering part of the voyage and indicated no real commitment to the Virginia settlers in spite of his sponsor's bond to Ralegh. Cocke may have expected the settlers to travel on the *Moonlight* instead of his ship. David Quinn also supposed that the sailors might not have wanted women settlers aboard as they could interfere with the privateering activities of the voyage.

The *Hopewell* sailed out of the Thames, with White aboard, followed by the other two ships. At Plymouth they found *Moonlight* unprepared to sail. After waiting for more than two weeks, they left *Moonlight* in port and sailed on March 20, 1590— so much for Ralegh's escort idea. *Moonlight* would not sail until early May. It would seem that White had ample time to contact Ralegh from Plymouth as he waited for the *Moonlight* to be made ready. However, he did not do so, and we are left wondering what would have happened if he had enlisted Ralegh's or Sanderson's help in resolving the issue of boarding the colonists on one or the other ship.

After a stop in Morocco, *Hopewell* and the other two ships passed the Canaries, and Captain Newport aboard *Little John* captured a large boatload of wine and spices. They reached Dominica on April 30, 1590. Newport stayed behind there to look for more prizes and caught up with the rest of the fleet again at Hispaniola (Haiti). They now had a Spanish pinnace they had captured near Puerto Rico and another Spanish cargo ship they had captured.

Surprisingly, the *Moonlight,* in company with *Conclude,* a pinnace of about thirty tons she had sailed with, caught up with the privateers at Tiburon on the southwest coast of Hispaniola. The fleet now numbered eight ships. It soon captured a ninth, a 300-ton ship called *El Buen Jesus*; but it needed repairs to plug the holes the English cannons had put in it. While Cocke had repairs made, Newport went off in pursuit of other Spanish merchantmen near Jamaica and then tailed the Mexican treasure galleys as they made their way slowly to Havana. Newport engaged one of the galleys in a sea battle and boarded it. In a fierce hand-to-hand battle on the deck of the galley, Newport lost his right arm to a Spanish cutlass blow. To make matters worse, the ship sank before they could recover the huge cargo of silver it contained. Understandably, Newport decided to sail back to England rather than continue with Cocke and his fleet. *Conclude* and *El Buen Jesus* sailed for England.

On July 27th Cocke turned his fleet north for the Florida passage. Bad weather slowed their progress and kept them well-offshore until August 9th. On August 15th, they anchored at Port Ferdinando. The winds continued to blow hard and the high seas made passage into the sound treacherous. On the next day White, Cocke and Spicer set out in the ships' boats but were diverted from Roanoke Island by smoke coming from one of the barrier islands.

They found no one there and decided to go to Roanoke Island on the next day. The fact that they spent so much time rowing into the sound and to one of the islands that they had to put off going to Roanoke Island for the next day gives some indication of how difficult it was for them to maneuver the clumsy ships' boats and make headway in the wind and high seas. On August 17th, they attempted a trip to Roanoke Island, but a huge wave crashed over Spicer's boat taking him and most of the men aboard to their death. Cocke's crew wanted to turn back, but White and Cocke urged them on. They didn't reach the island until nightfall, having taken all of the day to row perhaps twenty miles. They anchored off the north end of the island and blew horns and sang English songs hoping to attract the settlers. They saw a fire burning in the woods, but no one came to the shore.

In the morning of August 18th, they went ashore and, like Gonzalez who had been there more than two years before, they found no one. White saw Indian footprints in the sand, but no Indians showed themselves. At the settlement, he found CRO carved on a tree. On a post of a palisade that had been built around the dwellings, he read CROATOAN carved into the wood. The agreed upon sign of distress, the cross, was absent. So White concluded that some of the colonists must have gone south to live with Manteo's people. If the settlers had split up, those at Croatoan would know where the others had gone.

Someone had disassembled the houses. Iron bars, cannon balls and other heavy material lay inside the palisade, overgrown with weeds. White found that the settlers had left buried chests of belongings, apparently planning to retrieve them at some later time. Indians had dug up and ransacked those chests.

The Croatoan lived on the island south (left) of Roanoke

Among the debris, now spoiled by rain and mud, White found some of his own things he had entrusted to the settlers for safekeeping while he was gone. White said they continued to search the island but he reported finding nothing else. It isn't clear from the record how long they searched, but they left the island in time to row back to the ships that same day. Since it had taken them all the previous day to get to Roanoke, their search must not have lasted very long. White reported that the weather made it difficult for them to get back to the ships.

On August 19th with more favorable weather, they planned to sail *Hopewell* and *Moonlight* down to Croatoan Island to put White ashore to search for the Indians and the settlers. But that plan fell to the apparently still strong onshore winds that caused *Hopewell's* anchor cable to part and nearly drove the ship onto the shoals. After Cocke barely managed to make seaway and avoid disaster, he decided that they would sail to the Caribbean to replenish their water and supplies, layover there for the winter, and make a fresh start for Croatoan in the summer. That would also give him a chance to capture some more Spanish ships, of course.

Captain John Bedford, now in command of *Moonlight* as a result of Spicer's death, would have no part of that plan. His ship, he said, needed repairs; he had too few men. He sailed away for England—or so he said. The winds continued to plague *Hopewell,* making progress south painfully slow. Finally, desperate for water, they changed course for the Azores. At Flores (one of the islands of the Azores), White was shocked to find *Moonlight*; Captain Bedford hadn't limped home at all. He had gone on a privateering expedition. And perhaps no surprise, Sir John Hawkins was also there with other English ships poised to capture the Spanish treasure ships as they lumbered by loaded with gold and silver. But their timing was off; the Spanish Treasure fleet had already reached Spain, and none of the English ships found a prize at the Azores.

Hopewell brought a dejected John White back to Plymouth on October 24, 1590—wiser but unable to say where his settlers had gone or even if any of them still survived. White complained about the time Cocke wasted chasing prizes in the Caribbean, but he didn't fault him for his decision to abandon the plan to go to Croatoan. Apparently the weather on the Outer Banks when they were there made it nearly impossible to maneuver their ships close to the shore.

The investors, in this latest scheme of Ralegh's, lost interest when the final tally of prizes showed that they had lost a considerable amount of money. War with Spain would continue until 1604, and with the peace would come a renewed interest in an English colony in North America. But, for John White, the venture was ended. He would never have an opportunity to learn what had happened to his daughter, granddaughter or the other people of the Lost Colony, as it came to be called.

Ralegh would send out additional ships from time to time looking for traces of the Lost Colonists. Some would search along the Outer Banks while collecting medicinal plants; others would go to the Chesapeake Bay; but none returned with any clear evidence of what had happened to the settlers. However, Ralegh and others believed they had survived. Twenty years later, one goal of the Jamestown adventurers was to search for the lost Roanoke colonists. But, aside from the intelligence Captain John Smith would get from Powhatan, no one would obtain any concrete information about the Lost Colony.

How many people constitute the Lost Colony is difficult to pin down. When White sailed away in August of 1587, he left behind 115 men, women and children. But Grenville had left either fifteen or eighteen men behind (two were known killed) the year before, and when Drake evacuated Lane's colonists, he left three men on the mainland. That makes a total of 131 to 134. But, according to David Quinn, Drake may have left as many as 100 or more South American Indians and African slaves who were with him when his fleet suffered hurricane damage at the Outer Banks. Unfortunately, there is no documentary record of whether those Indians and slaves were still aboard when Drake rescued the colonists in 1586. Records indicate that Drake took them aboard in the Caribbean, and the records make no mention of him bringing them into England when he returned with the rescued colonists. But that doesn't provide sufficient information to conclude that Drake left the Indians and slaves at the Outer Banks. They could have been put ashore at any number of locations including St. Augustine where he destroyed the Spanish outpost.

With regard to John White's colonists, Quinn theorized that they probably split up, with some going to live with Manteo's people and the rest going to live with the Chesapeake Indians. To support the theory that some went to the Chesapeake, Quinn cited information in English archives indicating that Powhatan admitted to Captain John Smith that he had ordered the massacre of the Chesapeake Indian tribe and the English living with them. One reliable source of information is contained in William Strachey's *History of Travel in Virginia,* published soon after the alleged massacre. Strachey wrote:

> ...*that his Majesty hath been acquainted that the men, women and children of the first plantation at Roanoke were by practice and commandment of Powhatan (he himself persuaded there unto by his priests) miserably slaughtered without any offence given him.*

The massacre appeared to Quinn to have happened in 1607—twenty years after White left Roanoke Island. Virginia Dare would therefore have been old enough to have had children of her own, if she had lived that long. King James believed the massacre had occurred, and he ordered the execution of the Indian priests who had urged Powhatan to eradicate those people. The king's order was never carried out.

In Quinn's theory, the settlers at Croatoan would have known how to reach the other settlers and would have waited at Croatoan for the next ship from England to give the crew directions to the other colonists' location. We know that by June of 1588 the settlers had left Roanoke Island. The information from Gonzalez makes that clear. We also know that Manteo had remained friendly to the English and had even accepted their religion, so it seems likely that, in the absence of any distress signal in the message they left, the settlers had left Roanoke Island voluntarily and some, at least, had gone to Croatoan.

However, with regard to the remainder of the colonists who went elsewhere, there is some reason to dispute Quinn's linking of several separate accounts by Strachey to support his conclusion that the English and Chesapeake massacres were one-in-the-same. The information volunteered by Powhatan would seem to point to some English having gone north to the Chesapeake, since his authority did not extend as far as Roanoke Island or the adjoining mainland areas. If, however, Powhatan lied to Smith about killing the English colonists from Roanoke, it probably was to intimidate him by overstating his authority over Indian tribes south of the James River.

The most likely scenario has the English settlers being assimilated among the Indians living in present-day North Carolina and perhaps parts of Virginia. Whether or not Powhatan had a role in the massacre of the Roanoke Island colonists cannot be conclusively determined from the records available. In fact, we don't know for sure that any of the colonists left by John White were massacred, aside from George Howe who died in an Indian ambush while White was still on Roanoke Island.

One problem of the Lost Colonists being assimilated by the Indians has to do with disease. When the English came in contact with a tribe, disease and death followed soon after. The Indians came to associate living with the English with added risks of sickness and death. In fact, Harriot reported that

> *...within a few dayes after our departure...the people began to die very fast, and many in short space; in some townes about twentie, in some fourtie, in some sixtie, & in one sixe score* [120], *which in trueth was very manie in respect of their numbers.*

The Indians spoke of the invisible bullets that the English shot into them, bringing on sickness and death. Neither the English nor the Indians knew about germs and how disease could be transmitted from one person to another. To both cultures disease smacked of magic.

The Indians clearly made the link between the coming of the English and the coming of diseases. For that reason, the Indians may have been wary of living with large numbers of English. If they did so, based on Harriot's observations, it could have happened in time that the tribe became more English than Indian as far as their genetic makeup was concerned. In other words, in a combined tribe of say 200 Indians with about fifty English people, the number of Indians could have declined rather quickly to parity or even a minority of Indians due to the English diseases. Eventually, the surviving

Indians would have acquired immunity just as the English had. But by then, there could well have been more English survivors than Indians.

Other theories about the Lost Colonists have them: victims of a Spanish raid in which some were killed and others were taken to Spain to be tortured and killed by the Inquisition; killed by hostile Indians from the mainland; succumbing to drought or other natural disasters. Those theories seem implausible in the face of the absence of bodies when White searched the island, and, for that matter, modern searches have not found large numbers of skeletons from that era. One more plausible theory would be that the settlers were lost at sea. They had one pinnace, and they could have built additional small ships in the ten months they had before Gonzalez arrived. He even commented that he had found the slipway where they launched their boats. But it seems unlikely they would have put to sea with all 115 people in a couple of pinnaces unless it was to relocate to another spot reasonably close at hand—such as the Chesapeake Bay region.

The most logical conclusion seems to be that the Lost Colonists relocated initially to Croatoan, and perhaps other regions of North Carolina and, possibly, Virginia, where they became part of the various Indian tribes that inhabited the region. In time, they would have bred with the Indians and children would have been born of these mixed unions. Perhaps, twenty years after their departure from Roanoke Island, warriors dispatched by Powhatan attacked and killed some of the surviving colonists within modern-day North Carolina, although that seems unlikely. More likely, some English living with the Chesapeake may have died when Powhatan ordered his warriors to eradicate that tribe.

But some of the colonists must have survived—their presence was noted by John Smith and later Virginia colonists. Down through the generations, the mixture of Indian, English and perhaps African blood would have produced people with slightly different physical characteristics than the typical Algonquian Indians. That was known to have happened with other Europeans who found themselves abandoned or shipwrecked in North America, and it probably happened at Roanoke Island as well. For instance, Captain John Smith had an Indian guide named Mosco who clearly had some French or Spanish ancestry. Smith described Mosco as having a full beard.

Perhaps the best hope for unraveling this mystery is a combination of conventional archaeology and DNA analysis if human remains are ever found in an appropriate setting. Until then, the fate of the Lost Colonists will remain one of the great mysteries of the English Colonial period.

Chapter 13
Ralegh, Grenville and White after Roanoke Island

As previously discussed, the threat of Spanish invasion put many maritime plans on hold from 1587 to 1590 while Queen Elizabeth commandeered every available ship, soldier and mariner for the defense of her realm. Ralegh's role during that time was significant. He was responsible for the strategically important Cornish coast defense and took part in the naval engagement of the Spanish Armada. When not actively involved in fighting the Spanish, Ralegh divided his time between seeing to his plantations in Ireland and attending the queen at court. Ralegh should have gone to sea aboard the *Revenge* as Vice-Admiral of the English fleet sent to intercept the Spanish Treasure fleet as they sailed past the Azores on their way to Spain. However, Sir Richard Grenville took his place, much to Ralegh's good fortune. That English fleet encountered heavily armed Spaniards waiting for them at the Azores. Sir Richard Grenville was killed in that long and bloody battle in August, 1591.

That same year, Ralegh's attendance at court led to much more than he had anticipated. He had always enjoyed the company of the ladies of the court without getting entangled in a prospect of marriage. He had a daughter back in Ireland, but had not married the child's mother. But now, unaccountably, he fell in love with Bess Throckmorton, daughter of the queen's ambassador to the court of Paris. And soon Bess had to tell Walter that she was pregnant. They were secretly married in 1591. The marriage remained a secret for some months and eventually Bess gave birth to a baby boy named Damerei. Ralegh brought his son and the baby's nurse to Durham House. When in May, 1592, the queen found out about Ralegh's son and the secret marriage, she had Ralegh arrested and held for a short time in prison.

The solution to Ralegh's problem would have been to beg the queen's pardon for marrying without her permission, but Walter and Bess refused to stoop to that humiliation.

Consequently, Ralegh found himself out of favor for five years. Ralegh's first son died in infancy, but, a year later, Bess gave birth to their second son, Wat.

Ralegh lived the next couple of years as a country gentleman enjoying his wealth and watching Wat grow. Then, in 1595, he launched an extremely optimistic voyage to discover the mythical golden city of El Dorado, thought to be somewhere in the interior of Guyana. The Spaniards had sent several expeditions into Guyana in the 1580s looking unsuccessfully for the city where they believed hoards of gold were to be found.

Ralegh sailed with four ships and several hundred men to the West Indies where he destroyed a number of Spanish towns at the island of Trinidad, captured the Spanish governor, and then sailed on to the Orinoco River where he embarked on his exploration of the interior of Guyana. Guyana at that time was much bigger than the modern country of that name and encompassed the entire northeast portion of South America through which the Orinoco River flowed; much of it now part of Venezuela, Suriname and Brazil.

Ralegh's travels took him well into the interior where he found rocks that he mistakenly thought contained gold and silver. He also met with Indians who generally received him well—he and his men treated the Indians more kindly than the Spaniards had. But he found nothing of real value and, like the Spaniards, never found El Dorado. After a few weeks on this quest he returned to the coast, exchanged the Spanish governor for an English prisoner and sailed back to England with little accomplished except for the rich experiences that he put into his book titled *The discoveries of the large, rich and bewtiful empire of Guiana.*

While Ralegh had been exploring South America, the Spanish had actually attacked the English homeland and burned two villages in Cornwall. Queen Elizabeth agreed that it was time to launch another English assault on Spain and authorized a large fleet of more than 100 ships with 65,000 soldiers aboard to invade Spain at Cadiz. The command of the fleet was held by Admiral Lord Howard aboard *Ark Royal*, Robert Devereux the Earl of Essex—Queen Elizabeth's new favorite and Ralegh's rival—aboard *Duc Repulse*, and Vice-Admiral Sir Walter Ralegh aboard *Warspite*. They sailed into Cadiz on June 29, 1596, and Lord Howard foolishly ordered the soldiers into boats to row ashore. Some boats were overloaded and went down, drowning the heavily armored men. Seeing this, Ralegh lost his temper and had angry words with Lords Howard and Essex. At his urging they shifted into an attack on the Spanish ships in the harbor and a fierce, but effective, naval engagement ensued. Ralegh soon fell, his leg badly injured by fragments from his ship's deck splintered by a Spanish cannon ball.

Finally, the English soldiers stormed ashore and took the town. But the great wealth they hoped for was still aboard the Spanish ships in the harbor. As the English watched, the Spanish scuttled their own ships, sending them to the bottom of the harbor with untold riches that Ralegh could have put to good use. He had disposed of a great deal of his personal wealth in his expedition to South America and, to make matters worse, his plantations in Ireland and England were not producing as well as they should have due to widespread floods in the last years of the sixteenth century. Ralegh returned to England in June of 1597, injured but in better graces with Queen Elizabeth. Ralegh, Essex and Lord Howard led a subsequent attack on Spanish forces that turned out to be a debacle, with nothing more accomplished than Ralegh's successful raid on one of the islands of the Azores. This led to Essex's fall from favor in court, and he moved to Ireland.

By the end of the queen's reign, Ralegh had drawn the wrath of a number of influential men who were aligned with the soon to be King James I. Ralegh's patron, Queen Elizabeth, died on March 24, 1603, and one of his last official duties was to lead the Queen's Guards in her funeral cortege. In a subsequent meeting with King James, Ralegh was bluntly dismissed and soon lost many of his royal favors, including the Governorship of Jersey and Durham House in London. The King rightly understood that Ralegh still supported an aggressive policy toward Spain, and King James favored settling the peace as quickly as possible.

By November 17, 1603, Ralegh found himself dragged into the Court of the King's Bench, charged with multiple counts of treason. He made the classic mistake of attempting to defend himself, although the outcome would probably have been the same if he had hired a barrister to defend him. The idea that Ralegh had conspired with the Spanish to put another Stuart on the throne was ludicrous, but the jury returned a guilty verdict in a matter of minutes. Chief Justice Sir John Popham pronounced that Ralegh would be hanged, drawn and quartered for his alleged crime. On Ralegh's appeal, King James stayed the execution and ordered that Ralegh be held in the tower, pardoned but without his

liberty. He lived for thirteen years confined to two rooms in the Tower of London. Bess visited him there and gave birth to their third son, Carew in 1605. Ralegh also spent his time in the Tower writing his *History of the World* and other pieces that were eventually published.

Walter Ralegh and Bess in the Tower of London in one of his incarcerations

By 1616, King James had become desperate for money, and he was persuaded to think again about what Ralegh had written about El Dorado. On March 19, 1616, Ralegh found himself free from the tower and in command of a second expedition to Guyana. But this expedition was doomed from the start. The Spanish had been informed of Ralegh's plans, and the king had warned him that under no circumstances should he injure any Spaniard. The king expected Ralegh to go to Guyana (clearly held by the Spanish) and locate and exploit a gold mine, while not inconveniencing the Spanish in any way—truly a mission impossible.

Ralegh planned to get around this issue by using French Huguenots in any necessary aggression against the Spanish. He hoped that when he returned with his ships heaped with Spanish gold, the cash-strapped king would overlook any transgressions against the Spanish. In spite of many obstacles, Ralegh, now an old man (about 63), sailed from Plymouth on June 12, 1617 with ten ships. His son Wat commanded Ralegh's flagship, aptly named *Destiny*. They were beset by storms and illness, and consequently made an extremely slow crossing from the Canaries to Trinidad, arriving there on November 14th. The Huguenots never arrived.

When the now all-English operation began, Ralegh remained on board his ship, too ill to take part in the expedition ashore. He relied on others to secure the area of the supposed mine, which was near a Spanish fort, and to work the mine and bring back what they could. The inevitable happened. The Englishmen, with Wat Ralegh in the vanguard, stormed into the fortified Spanish San Thomé, sacked the village, killed the Spanish governor, and then discovered that there was no gold mine. Even more tragic, Wat Ralegh died instantly from a musket ball in the first charge on the town. Ralegh's brother George then led an expedition up the Oronoco, following in Sir Walter's footsteps, and came back equally empty handed. A sick and grieving Sir Walter Ralegh heard the account of Wat's death and the attack on the Spaniards. He was a dead man. All that remained was the trip back to

England and the executioner's axe, which fell and ended Ralegh's life on October 29, 1618.

As for Governor John White, little is known about his life after his last voyage to Roanoke Island in 1590. John White lived about fifty-three years (ca. 1545 to 1598). lebame houston speculated that John White gave up on his hopes to find the "Lost Colonists" after his voyage in 1590. She wrote

After White's return to England, he retired from colonization and settled in Ireland— presumably alone. He died in 1598, at the age of about 53, without ever having made another effort to locate his daughter, granddaughter and colonists, and without ever becoming the colonial governor of his fantasies. New evidence strongly suggests that his wife Thomasine pre-deceased him in 1590/91, as did at least two of his grandchildren.

The grandchildren houston referred to were two children of Ananias and Elenor Dare who remained in England when their parents sailed with John White to Roanoke Island in 1587. Their names were Ananias and Thomasine.

Chapter 14
Roanoke Island in Later Years

In spite of several separate searches by colonists at Jamestown, traces of the Lost Colonists still eluded them. Two men sent by Captain John Smith returned in 1608 from present-day North Carolina with a story that they were told there were four survivors of the Powhatan massacre of the Lost Colonists living there. But no surviving Lost Colonists ever found their way back to English society in Jamestown. John Pory, Secretary of Virginia in 1619, went south of the James River to the area near the Chowan and Roanoke Rivers where rumors indicated the survivors had gone. He found no sign of English people living there. Most peculiarly, none of the searches undertaken by people from Jamestown focused on Roanoke Island or Croatoan.

However, on May 8, 1654, Francis Yeardley, a Virginia planter who was living at Lynnhaven (now part of Virginia Beach), sent a letter to John Ferrar in England in which he described how eight months before he had come to meet the "great commander of those parts [Roanoke Island]." The Indians living at Roanoke Island "shewed them [fur traders] the ruins of Sir Walter Ralegh's fort" and presented them a relic from the place they returned to Yeardley. He didn't identify what kind of relic it was. The letter gives no indication that the Indians at Roanoke Island knew any more about the Lost Colonists than Yeardley did. But they clearly knew that the English had a settlement there a couple generations before their time. What became of the Lost Colonists remained a mystery.

Nothing more appears in the records until John Lawson's account of his visit to the Outer Banks and Roanoke Island in 1701. He wrote:

The first Discovery and Settlement of this Country was by the Procurement of Sir Walter Raleigh, in Conjunction with some Publick-spirited Gentlemen of that Age, under the Protection of Queen Elizabeth; for which Reason it was then named Virginia, being begun on that Part called Ronoak-Island, where the Ruins of a Fort are to be seen at this day, as well as some old English Coins which have been lately found; and a Brass-Gun, a Powder-Horn, and one small Quarter deck-Gun, made of Iron Staves, and hoop'd with the same Metal; which Method of making Guns might very probably be made use of in those Days, for the Convenience of Infant-Colonies.

A farther Confirmation of this we have from the Hatteras Indians, who either then lived on Ronoak-Island, or much frequented it. These tell us that several of their Ancestors were white People, and could talk in a Book, as we do; the Truth of which is confirm'd by gray Eyes being found frequently amongst these Indians, and no others. They value themselves extremely for their Affinity to the English, and are ready to do them all friendly Offices. It is probable that this Settlement miscarry'd for want of timely Supplies from England; or thro' the Treachery of the Natives, for we may reasonably suppose that the English were forced to cohabit with them, for Relief and Conversation; and that in process of Time, they conform'd themselves to the Manners of their Indian Relations. And thus we see, how apt Humane Nature is to degen-erate.

John Lawson had traveled extensively among the Indians of the Carolinas by the time he wrote this. We should therefore take as authoritative his statement about the English features of the Indians he found living around Roanoke Island. And that shouldn't be surprising if, in the course of their assimilation among the Indians, the English diseases decimated the Indian population putting them in the minority among a mixed community of English and Indians. The following Indian legend of Ralegh's ghost ship that Lawson repeated reinforces his comment that the Indians of that area had an affinity for their English heritage:

I cannot forbear inserting here a pleasant Story that passes for an uncontested Truth amongst the Inhabitants of this Place; which is, that the Ship which brought the first Colonies, does often appear amongst them, under Sail, in a gallant Posture, which they call Sir Walter Raleigh's Ship; And the truth of this has been affirm'd to me, by Men of the best Credit in the Country.

By the time of Lawson's visit, a number of events had affected England and North America. In the middle of the seventeenth century, England had experienced a civil war and King James's successor had been executed, ushering in a repressive government that was eventually replaced by another Stuart, King Charles II. During the Commonwealth period following the civil war, Virginia planter Francis Yeardley acquired Roanoke Island and arranged for the Indians there to move inland. He paid £200 for the land, which consisted of far more than just Roanoke Island, and he also had carpenters build an English-style house for the Indian chief or emperor as Yeardley called him. English settlers from the James River watershed then began to occupy Roanoke Island once more.

Under King Charles II, successor to the Commonwealth government, the province of Carolina was carved out of Virginia. Grants of land on the island followed the charter in 1663. Roanoke Island, situated near the main entrance into Albemarle Sound, took on new prominence and was considered as a site for the capital of the new English province and a major port. Mariners, harbor pilots and farmers made up the residents of Roanoke Island during the last quarter of the seventeenth century. However, the shifting sands of the Outer Banks eventually began to close the Roanoke Inlet, and by 1730, the idea of a port on the island proved impractical.

A confederation of Tuscarora and other Indians from the mainland attacked settlers on Roanoke Island in 1711 and 1713. The English drove the Indians well into the interior of Carolina in 1714 and negotiated a peace treaty with them. Life on Roanoke Island continued peacefully, with cattle roaming freely and settlers unaffected by events beyond the island until the colonies declared their independence from Britain. During the Revolutionary War, British troops came to the island to steal cattle and other food supplies as they did at many other undefended coastal or tidewater locations.

During the nineteenth century, life on Roanoke Island for the growing population continued to be one of isolation and self-sufficiency, residents depending on their crops, livestock and the seafood they gathered. The population of the island in the

1850 census was listed as 610 (140 of those were slaves).

Map of Civil War fortifications on Roanoke Island

With the onset of the Civil War, the island took on a new importance. It appeared an ideal location for a fort to control commerce through the sounds. The Confederate forces took control of the island first and constructed three forts on the northern end: Fort Huger, Fort Blanchard and Fort Bartow. These forts consisted of earthen embankments and cannons facing the approaches to the island. They also built two smaller defensive earthworks: one near Shallowbag Bay on the east side of the island, and one called Fort Russell in the center of the island facing south. In February 1862, Union General Ambrose Burnside came with a massive flotilla of small ships, barges, steamers, and 7,500 troops. He invaded and took the island, capturing 2,675 Confederate soldiers. That marked the end of the fighting on Roanoke Island.

During the Civil War, escaped slaves flocked to Roanoke Island once it fell under Union control. General Burnside established a superintendent with responsibility for the former slaves, and some found employment as servants for the army. These freed slaves received rations and clothing and earned wages for their labors for the first time. Some also worked building coastal forts for the army and docks at Roanoke Island. In 1862, the influx brought the Island population up to 1,000.

A year later, a colony for freedmen existed on the northern end of the island. Much of the funds and materials needed to build the colony came from the Freedman's Associations in Boston and New York. Surveyors laid out a town following the typical gridiron plan with long avenues named after Lincoln and Burnside, with numerical and alphabetical cross-streets (First Street, A Street, etc.). Each householder had to build a house and cultivate a garden to qualify for one of the one-acre lots. By the beginning of 1865, the town included 591 or more houses and 3,000 people. They had a church, schools, warehouses and mills. Unfortunately, the Freedmen's Colony failed to prosper for at least two reasons: the promised wages often weren't paid, leaving the residents in poverty; and so many able-bodied black men had been inducted for service into the Union Army, there were insufficient men left to work at the trades there. One estimate had the Federal Government owing the Freedmen's Colony residents more than $18,000 by the end of the war.

The Freedmen's Bureau was established to assist former slaves

Following the end of the war, the former land owners and residents of Roanoke Island returned and claimed their property. By the end of 1866, only about one-half of the Freedmen's Colony residents remained. The Federal Freedmen's Bureau (set up by the government to ensure the successful transition of the former slaves into society and their fair treatment by white employers) ended the process of providing rations to the residents and advised returning all the island property to the former owners as a way to force the Freedmen's Colony residents off the island. The Freedmen's Bureau supposed this move would induce the people to seek better employment elsewhere. Within a few months most of the freedmen had left the island, leaving very few behind. But descendants of those few still live on Roanoke Island.

In 1870, the North Carolina General Assembly created a new county—Dare County—with Roanoke Island at its center. The town of Manteo, near Wingina's palisaded village and near where the original English Colony settled, became the county seat and incorporated in 1899. At the end of the nineteenth century, fishing employed most Roanoke Island residents. But tourism had become an adjunct of the economy of Dare County with the development of hunting clubs on the Outer Banks. These clubs brought outsiders into the area at certain times of the year. By 1900, Roanoke Island held about 3,000 residents.

At the beginning of the twentieth century, various scientific experiments were carried out in Dare County and at Roanoke Island. The Wright Brothers developed early aircraft technology there taking advantage of the strong and steady winds over the dunes of the Outer Banks. Also R. A. Fessenden, a former employee of Thomas A. Edison, installed electronic equipment at Roanoke Island, Cape Hatteras, and Cape Henry in Virginia. His experiments led to technical advancements in wireless communication of voice, data and music.

Although various dignitaries, including President Monroe, visited the ruins of the English fort on the north end of the island, little was done to preserve it until late in the nineteenth century. By that time, people referred to the site as Fort Raleigh, which continues to designate the site of the original settlement. In 1894, Edward Graham Daves and like-minded North Carolina natives formed the Roanoke Colony Memorial Association and acquired over 260 acres from the owners of the settlement lands, including the fort site. The association met for the first time at Manteo where they arranged for a caretaker to oversee and prevent further vandalism or looting of artifacts from the site. A year later, Talcott Williams from the University of Pennsylvania conducted archaeological tests of the site that confirmed the presence of remnants of the fort of the early colonial period. Monuments to Virginia Dare and Sir Walter Ralegh were erected during the next twenty years, but the Association had to sell off much of the land to service the debt they had incurred. In spite of all their efforts and an eventual federal appropriation of funds, the Association managed only to erect some more commemorative plaques and pillars marking the entrance to the site.

In 1934, the Roanoke Colony Memorial Association donated the Fort Raleigh lands to the State of North Carolina, which began well-intentioned but misguided reconstruction of the settlement, starting with building log cabins. Five years later, the National Park Service, after several years of negotiations, took over responsibility for the Fort Raleigh site. During that period and continuing through the war years, the Roanoke Island Historical Association produced the unique outdoor drama, *The Lost Colony*, written by Paul Green, and they undertook projects to stabilize the shoreline near the site.

From 1947 onward, the National Park Service has managed the site and has steadily added to our knowledge of what took place there during the critical years of 1584 through 1590 by extensive archaeological explorations, archival research, and other studies. They have also reacquired much of the land sold by the Roanoke Colony Memorial Association and have installed a reconstruction of the original fort erected by Ralph Lane. Their work continues and, undoubtedly, the interpretation of the site will continue to evolve as archaeologists, historians and other specialists reveal new information about how those sixteenth century English colonists lived, what they brought with them, what they built, and how they occupied the site. More than a quarter of a million visitors from all over the world visit Fort Raleigh each year, learning about the first serious English settlement attempt in North America and taking home a new understanding about life in the wilderness during Elizabethan times. The population of Roanoke Island in 2000 was nearly 7,000 people.

Although most traces of the settlers landed at Roanoke Island in the years 1584 through 1587 have disappeared, what they contributed to this country has not. They pioneered English settlement in North America. Their trials taught valuable lessons that would be advantageous to later colonists in Virginia and New England.

When the Virginia Company sent the first 104 settlers to Jamestown in 1606, they had the advantage of Thomas Harriot's published work and the knowledge that he had gained from his association with men such as Manteo and Wanchese. He had passed on valuable information regarding what crops they could rely on, how to communicate with the Indians, and what trade goods would be most useful to take to America.

The Roanoke Island settlers had determined that the Chesapeake Bay would be a better haven for English ships—safer from Spanish raids and safer to navigate in the ships of the day. They also knew how critical to their survival the Indians would be.

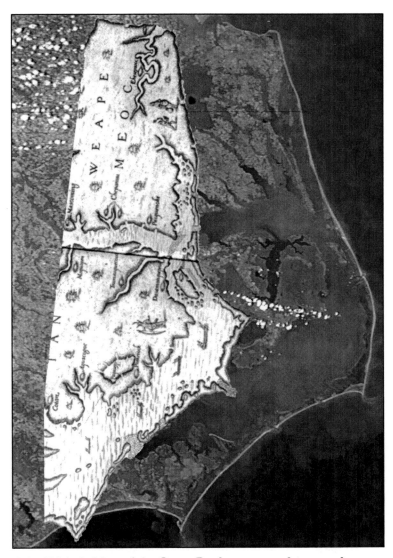

John White's Map of the Outer Banks compared to a modern satellite image. Note the relatively accurate placement of the prominent capes. White had no way to accurately determine longitude, so the east-west position of some features are distorted. Nonetheless, his map was an excellent effort.

This hard-learned information obtained by the Roanoke Island settlers didn't prevent subsequent colonists from making some of the same mistakes in the Chesapeake or New England, but they had been forewarned. The maps that Harriot and White produced remained the best navigational aids available for many years. Their maps were blended into Captain John Smith's map of Virginia which expanded English knowledge of the Mid-Atlantic region north to the limits of the Chesapeake Bay and west to the rapids of the major rivers flowing into the bay.

The Roanoke Island colonial attempts by Ralegh and White were short-term failures but paved the way for the later, successful venture of the Virginia Company of London. It may be that the competing goal of privateering doomed the Roanoke ventures. The goal of the Roanoke Island settlement was vague to be sure. However, the concept of the City of Ralegh—to establish a permanent settlement in the Chesapeake Bay region in which adventurers would also be landowners—predated the subsequent establishment of a similar land transfer to Virginia adventurers by forty years. Had Governor White been able to land his colonists at a Chesapeake Bay location instead of Roanoke Island in 1587, the City of Ralegh would have had as good a chance for success as the Jamestown Island settlement of 1607. The concept was sound; it offered the incentive of land ownership to an appropriate mix of adventurers, artisans, farmers and families motivated to work together, willing to risk all on the venture and make the gamble a success. Their likely destination on the southern shore of the James River would have seen them settled among Indians whom they expected, based on prior experience, to be supportive. Those Indians were not under Powhatan's thrall and could have provided a more secure haven for the English than Jamestown Island afforded the settlers nearly twenty years later.

As to the ultimate fate of those early settlers left by Ralegh and White, hopefully, continued scientific and archival work will reveal more about the roughly 130 individuals known to have been abandoned at Roanoke Island: where they went and what became of them. Until that time, the saga of the Lost Colonists will continue to pique our imagination.

Notes

p. 8. "To say simply that English piracy flourished..."
Isil, Olivia with houston, lebame and Dough, Wynne, *Piracy, Privateering and Elizabethan Maritime Expansion* (Internet Site: National Park Service, Roanoke Revisited Heritage Education Program, www.nps.gov/fora/piracy.htm), p. 3.

p. 12, 13. "[John] Rastell, a printer and publisher by trade..."
Noel Hume, Ivor, *The Virginia Adventure: Roanoke to Jamestown: an Archaeological and Historical Odyssey* (Charlottesville: University Press of Virginia, 1994) p. 7, 8.

p. 20. "The first discovery of these coasts (never heard of before) was well begun by John Cabot the father, and Sebastian his son, an Englishman born, who were the first..."
Hayes, Edward, *A Report of the Voyage and success thereof, attempted in the year of our Lord 1583 by Sir Humphrey Gilbert, knight*, contained in *Hakluyt's Voyages*, edited by Richard David (Boston: Houghton Mifflin Company, 1981), p. 301, 302.

p. 22. "Be content, we have seen enough, and take no care of expense past, I will set you forth royally the next spring..."
Ibid. p. 324.

p. 28. "The Galeons were 64 in number, being of an huge bigness..."
Hakluyt, Richard, *Hakluyt's Voyages*, contained in *Everyman's Library*, edited by Ernest Rhys (London: J. M. Dent & Sons, Ltd., 1907), Volume 2, pages 372, 373.

p. 33. "...a reputation as a proud, hot-tempered, and imperious man..."
Quinn, David Beers, *Set Fair for Roanoke, Voyages and Colonies, 1584-1606* (Chapel Hill and London: University of North Carolina Press, 1985), p. 6.

p. 35. "Many voyages have been pretended [tried], yet hitherto never any thoroughly..." Hayes, Edward, *A Report of the Voyage and success thereof, attempted in the year of our Lord 1583 by Sir Humphrey Gilbert, knight*, contained in

Hakluyt's Voyages, edited by Richard David (Boston: Houghton Mifflin Company, 1981), p. 301.

p. 37. "was more like the climate in border regions of Canada..."
 Loker, Aleck, *Chesapeake Bay, Witnesses to the Creation* (Leonardtown, Md.: St. Clement's Island-Potomac River Museum, 2002), p. 7.

p. 42. "the greatest Wiroans that we had dealing with..."
Harriot, Thomas, *A Briefe and True Report of the New Found Land of Virginia,* Rosenwald Collection Reprint Series (New York: Dover Publications, Inc., 1972), p. 25.

p. 45. "English ministers often doubled as healers"
Kupperman, Karen Ordahl, *Indians and English: Facing off in Early America* (Ithaca, New York: Cornell University Press, 2000) p. 132.

p. 47. "...the initial contact with Europeans in the [sixteenth] century..."
Loker, Aleck, *Chesapeake Bay, Witnesses to the Creation* (Leonardtown, Md.: St. Clement's Island-Potomac River Museum, 2002), p. 2.

p. 49. "Elizabeth by the grace of God of England, France and Ireland Queene, ..."
Queen Elizabeth of England, *The letters patents, graunted by the Queenes Majestie to Master Walter Ralegh, now Knight, for the discovering and planting of new lands and Countries, to continue the space of 6. yeeres and no more*, contained in *The Roanoke Voyages, 1584-1590*, edited by David Beers Quinn, (London: Hakluyt Society, 1955) volume I, p. 82-89.

p. 50. "the fift part of all the oare of golde and silver..."
Ibid.

p. 51. "Englishmen may have sighted Newfoundland as early as the 1480s,..."
Quinn, David Beers, *Set Fair for Roanoke, Voyages and Colonies, 1584-1606* (Chapel Hill and London: University of North Carolina Press, 1985), p. 12.

p. 52. "In 1566 a Spanish expedition formally annexed the Outer Banks,..."
Ibid., p. 13.

p. 52. "Discourse of Western Planting"
Hakluyt, Richard, *Discourse of Western Planting*, edited by David B. Quinn and Alison M. Quinn, (London: Hakluyt Society, 1993).

p. 54. "west of England."
Barlowe, Philip, *The first voyage made to the coasts of America, with two barks, where in were Captaines M. Philip Amadas, and M. Arthur Barlowe, who discovered part of the Countrey now called Virginia, Anno 1584* contained in *Hakluyt's Voyages*, edited by Richard David (Boston: Houghton Mifflin Company, 1981), p. 445.

p. 55. "...and after thankes given to God for our safe arrivall thither,..."
Ibid. p. 446.

p. 56, 57. "...gave him a shirt, a hat & some other things,... "
Ibid. p. 447.

p. 57. "What pretty clothes you ..."
Norman, Charles, *Discoverers of America: A Wilderness Continent Seen Through the Eyes of the First Explorers* (New York: Thomas Y. Crowell Company, 1968), p. 188.

p. 58. "When English venturers looked at America's natives..."
Kupperman, Karen Ordahl, *Indians and English: Facing off in Early America* (Ithaca, New York: Cornell University Press, 2000) p. 75.

p. 60. "pidgin"
Ibid., p. 86.

p. 62. "Theatrum Orbis Terrarum"
Ortelius, Abraham, *Theatrum Orbis Terrarum*, (Antwerp : Diesth, Aegid, 1570) Americae Sive Novi Orbis.

p. 65. "that no Indian be forced to labor unwillingly."
Quinn, David Beers, *Set Fair for Roanoke, Voyages and Colonies, 1584-1606* (Chapel Hill and London: University of North Carolina Press, 1985), p. 47.

p. 65. "...we will proceed with extremity, conquer, fortify and plant..."
Ibid., p. 50.

p. 73. "intolerable pride and insatiable ambition."
Ibid., p. 66.

p. 85, 86. "...the supply of our necessities..."
Ibid., p. 134.

p. 88. "...they left all things so confusedly,..."
Hakluyt, Richard, *The third voyage made by a ship sent in the yeere 1586, to the reliefe of the Colony planted in Virginia, at the sole charges of Sir Walter Ralegh,* contained in *The Roanoke Voyages, 1584-1590,* edited by David Beers Quinn, (London: Hakluyt Society, 1955) volume I, p. 478.

p. 88. "[the venture's] bias on the military side emphasized the colony's position as an outpost..."
Quinn, David Beers, *Set Fair for Roanoke, Voyages and Colonies, 1584-1606* (Chapel Hill and London: University of North Carolina Press, 1985), p. 96.

p. 88. "...primarily an experiment..."
Ibid., p. 97.

p. 93, 94. "No area of eastern North America was so thoroughly examined..."
Ibid., p. 157.

p. 94. "A brief and True Report of the new found land..."
Harriot, Thomas, *A Briefe and True Report of the New Found Land of Virginia,* Rosenwald Collection Reprint Series (New York: Dover Publications, Inc., 1972).

p. 95. "...no student of his [Fernandez] personality and actions..."
Quinn, David Beers, *Set Fair for Roanoke, Voyages and Colonies, 1584-1606* (Chapel Hill and London: University of North Carolina Press, 1985), p. 258.

p. 100. "...the summer was far spent wherefore he would land all the planters..."
Ibid., p. 279.

p. 107. "God justly punishing our former theeverie..."
Quinn, David B. and Quinn, Alison M. editors, *Virginia Voyages from Hakluyt* (London: Oxford University Press, 1973) p. 114.

p. 117. "...that his Majesty hath been acquainted, that the men, women, and children..."
Strachey, William, *The Historie of Travell into Virginia Britania*, edited by Louis B. Wright and Virginia Freund (London: Hakluyt Society, 1953), v. 103, p. 91.

p. 119. "...within a few days after our departure...the people began to die very fast,..."
Harriot, Thomas, *A Briefe and True Report of the New Found Land of Virginia*, Rosenwald Collection Reprint Series (New York: Dover Publications, Inc., 1972), p. 28.

p. 124. "The discoveries of the large, rich and bewtiful empyre of Guiana"
Ralegh, Sir Walter, *The discoveries of the large, rich and bewtiful empire of Guiana* (London: R. Robinson, 1596).

p. 126. "The History of the World"
Ralegh, Sir Walter, *The History of the World*, (London: W. Burre, 1614).

p. 128. "After White's return to England..."
houston, lebame, *John White, "traveling artist"*, (Manteo, NC: Roanoke Island Historical Association, The Lost Colony, Theater Under the Stars, 2005 Souvenir Program, 2005), p. 11.

p. 129. "great commander of those parts" and "shewed them the ruins of Sir Walter Ralegh's fort"
Yeardley, Francis, *Narratives of Early Carolina, 1650-1708, Narratives of Early Carolina, 1650-1708,* edited by Alexander S. Salley, Jr. (New York: Barnes and Noble, 1967), p. 25, 26.

p. 130, 131. "The first Discovery and Settlement of this Country…"
Lawson, John, *A New Voyage to Carolina,* edited by Hugh Talmage Lefler, (Chapel Hill: University of North Carolina Press, 1967), p. 62.

p. 131. "I cannot forbear inserting here, a pleasant Story… "
Ibid., p. 62.

Sir Walter Raleigh's Lost Colonists

The names of all the men, women, and children known to have been on the 1587 voyage. Note, some such as Simon Fernando (Fernandez) did not remain on Roanoke Island.

Men	Men
John White, Governor	Thomas Smith
Roger Bailie, Assistant	Richard Kemme
Ananias Dare, Assistant	Thomas Harris
Christopher Cooper, Assistant	Richard Taverner
Thomas Stevens, Assistant	John Earnest
John Sampson, Assistant	Henry Johnson
Dyonis Harvie, Assistant	John Starte
Roger Prat, Assistant	Richard Darige
George Howe, Assistant	William Lucas
Simon Fernando, Assistant	Arnold Archard
Nicholas Johnson	John Wright
Thomas Warner	William Dutton
Anthony Cage	Morris Allen
John Jones	William Waters
John Tydway	Richard Arthur
Ambrose Viccars	John Chapman
Edmond English	William Clement
Thomas Topan	Robert Little
Henry Berrye	Hugh Tayler
Richard Berrye	Richard Wildye
John Spendlove	Lewes Wotton
John Hemmington	Michael Bishop
Thomas Butler	Henry Browne
Edward Powell	Henry Rufoote
John Burden	Richard Tomkins
James Hynde	Henry Dorrell
Thomas Ellis	Charles Florrie
William Browne	Henry Mylton
Michael Myllet	Henry Payne
	Thomas Harris
	William Nicholes
	Thomas Phevens

Men	Women & Children
John Borden	Elyoner Dare
Thomas Scot	Margery Harvie
William Willes	Agnes Wood
John Brooke	Wenefrid Powell
Cutbert White	Joyce Archard
John Bright	Jane Jones
Clement Tayler	Elizabeth Glane
William Sole	Jane Pierce
John Cotsmur	Audry Tappan
Humfrey Newton	Alis Chapman
Thomas Colman	Emme Merrimoth
Thomas Gramme	.... Colman
Marke Bennet	Margaret Lawrence
John Gibbes	Joan Warren
John Stilman	Jane Mannering
Robert Wilkinson	Rose Payne
Peter Little	Elizabeth Viccars
John Wyles	
Brian Wyles	**Children**
George Martyn	John Sampson
Hugh Pattenson	Robert Ellis
Martyn Sutton	Ambrose Viccars
John Farre	Thomas Archard
John Bridger	Thomas Humfrey
Griffen Jones	Tomas Smart
Richard Shaberdge	George Howe
James Lasie	John Prat
Thomas Hewet	William Wythers
William Berde	
John Cheven	**Born on Roanoke Island**
	Virginia Dare
	.... Harvie

Image Credits

Cover. Image adapted from John White's Map of Virginia (see credit for page 80)

P. 11. A portion of Americae sive quartae orbis parties nova et exactissima descriptio, Map by Diego Gutiérrez, 1562. Map Collections, 1500-2004. American Memory. Library of Congress.

P. 14. The Concept of the New World in the Mid-16th Century. Drawing by author.

P. 26. Sir Francis Drake, Prints and Photographs Collections, Library of Congress, reproduction number LC-USZ62-38479.

P. 29. Armada Image combined from images 59 and 60, Description & representation de toutes les victoires tant par eau que par terre, lesquelles Dieu a octroiees aux nobles, hauts & puissants seigneurs, messeignrs. les Estats des Provinces vnies du Païs-Bas, souz la conduite & gouuernement de Son Excellence, le prince Mavrice de Nassav, published in Leyden 1612. The Kraus Collection of Sir Francis Drake, Library of Congress.

P. 32. Sir Walter Ralegh engraving by Simon van de Passe, Holland. , Prints and Photographs Collections, Library of Congress, reproduction number LC-USZ62-2951.

P. 37. Outer Banks of North Carolina, Satellite Image of the North Carolina coast courtesy of MODIS Rapid Response Project at the National Aeronautics and Space Administration (NASA) Goddard Space Flight Center (GSFC).

P. 39. A Weroance (Leader) of a Virginia Indian Tribe Image 49 from Das sechste Theil Americae oder Der Historien Hieron. Benzo das dritte Buch. Darinnen erzehlet wirt, wie die Spanier die..., published in Oppenheim, 1620. The Kraus Collection of Sir Francis Drake, Library of Congress.

P. 41. Indian Woman, cropped from Image 52, ibid.

P. 42. The Village of Pomeiooc, cropped from Image 70, ibid.

P. 44. Indians placed their dead..., cropped from Image 74, ibid.

p. 51. Detail from Spanish Map of 1562, cropped and enhanced from Americae sive quartae orbis parties nova et exactissima descriptio, Map by Diego Gutiérrez, 1562. Map Collections, 1500-2004. American Memory. Library of Congress.

P. 56. Indian Dugout Canoe, cropped from Image 60, Das sechste Theil Americae oder Der Historien Hieron. Benzo das dritte Buch. Darinnen erzehlet wirt, wie die Spanier die..., published in Oppenheim, 1620. The Kraus Collection of Sir Francis Drake, Library of Congress.

P. 60. Thomas Harriot. Author's sketch after the portrait of Thomas Harriot in the collection of Trinity College, Oxford University.

P. 64. Sir Richard Grenville. Aauthor's sketch after the portrait of Richard Grenville in the collection of the National Portrait Gallery, London.

P. 68. The typical route to and from America. Drawing by author.

P. 72. A chief of the Roanoke, possibly Wingina, cropped from Image 53, Das sechste Theil Americae oder Der Historien Hieron. Benzo das dritte Buch. Darinnen erzehlet wirt, wie die Spanier die..., published in Oppenheim, 1620. The Kraus Collection of Sir Francis Drake, Library of Congress.

P. 75. John White's drawing of Roanoke Island, cropped from Image 48, ibid.

P. 80. John White's Map of Virginia, combined from Images 5 and 6, ibid.

P. 83. The English depended on the Indians for their food, Image 62, ibid.

P. 114. The Croatoan lived on the island south of Roanoke, detail from illustration on P. 80.

P. 126. Walter Ralegh and Bess in the Tower of London, Prints and Photographs Collections, Library of Congress, reproduction number LC-USZC4-669.

p. 133. Map of Civil War fortifications on Roanoke Island. Adapted from Abbott, John S. C. "The Navy in the North Carolina Sounds," Harper's new monthly magazine, v. 32, Dec. 1865 to May 1866. p. 575.

P. 135. The Freedmen's Bureau was established to assist former slaves, Prints and Photographs Collections, Library of Congress, reproduction number LC-USz62-105555.

P. 139. Comparison of White map and modern image. Composite image incorporating detail from image on pages 37 and 80. Note scale of White map adjusted to fit the scale of the satellite image.

INDEX

156

162

White, John 40, 41,
        66, 73, 75, 79,
        80, 87, 88, 93-
        95, 97-107,
        109-111, 119,
        120, 128, 140,
        141, 146, 148,
        150, 152
White, Thomasine 128
Wildye, Richard 148
Wilkinson, Robert 149
Willes, William   149
Williams, Talcott 137
Williamsburg, VA   iv,
        46
Wingandacoa 57
Wingina (Pemisapan)
        57, 71, 72, 74,
        75, 81-85, 101,
        136, 151
Wococon 71, 74, 80
Wood, Agnes 149
Woodland Culture 39
Wotton, Lewes 148
Wright Brothers 136
Wright, John 148
Wyles, Brian 149
Wyles, John 149
Wythers, William 149

Y-
Yeardley, Francis 129,
        131, 132, 147
Youghal, Ireland 93
Yucatan 12

Printed in the United States
221327BV00005B/2/P

9 781928 874089